PEACE, DEVELOPMENT AND COMMUNITY

The Look East Imagination of India with Special Reference to Northeast India

PEACE, DEVELOPMENT AND COMMUNITY

The Look East Imagination of India with Special Reference to Northeast India

IMANKALYAN LAHIRI

Maulana Abul Kalam Azad Institute of Asian Studies
Kolkata

in association with

KNOWLEDGE WORLD

KW Publishers Pvt Ltd
New Delhi

The **Maulana Abul Kalam Azad Institute of Asian Studies** (MAKAIAS) is an autonomous body under the Ministry of Culture, Government of India. Based in Kolkata, it was registered as a Society under the West Bengal Registration of Societies' Act of 1961 on the 4th of January 1993, with Prof. Nurul Hasan, the then Governor of West Bengal, as the President of the Society. It is funded by the Department of Culture, Government of India.

MAKAIAS is a centre for research and learning with a focus on social, cultural, economic and political / administrative developments in Asia from the middle of the 19th Century onwards, with special emphasis on their links with India, and also on the life and works of Maulana Abul Kalam Azad.

ISBN 978-93-86288-33-2 Hardback
ISBN 978-93-86288-34-9 ebook

Published in India by Kalpana Shukla

KNOWLEDGE WORLD

KW Publishers Pvt Ltd
4676/21, First Floor, Ansari Road
Daryaganj, New Delhi 110002
Phone: +91 11 23263498/43528107
Marketing: kw@kwpub.com
Editorial: jose@kwpub.com
Website: www.kwpub.com

2011 FIP BA BEST PUBLISHERS AWARD (ENGLISH)

Printed and Bound by Bhavish Graphics.

CONTENTS

PREFACE

This work is the outcome of the Project entitled: *Peace, Development and Community: The Look East Imagination of India with Special Reference to Northeast India* sponsored by Maulana Abul Kalam Azad Institute of Asian Studies (MAKAIAS), Kolkata.

It took almost one year to complete this project. The research area is very vast to complete in a year, however, efforts were made to complete a pilot study on the project theme to arrive at certain conclusions. A large number of secondary and primary documents have been referred to while writing this project and, at the same time, several field surveys have been conducted both in formal and in informal ways. Two major field visits have been conducted during this one year of writing this project, one was in Imphal (Moreh-Tamu Border) and the other was at Aizawl including Champhai (Zokhawthar-Rhi Border). During this one year two major seminars have been conducted in Kolkata by inviting scholars and journalists from the Northeastern Region. A one-day seminar was conducted on March 21, 2015 where Rajeev Bhattacharyya, renowned Guwahati-based journalist and Dr. Suraj L. Singh, a renowned scholar from D. M. College of Arts, Manipur and who is also associated with this project, shared their views on India's Look East Policy concerning Peace, Development and Connectivity of the region. A special lecture was arranged by the Jadavpur Association of International Relations (JAIR) on India's Act East Policy on February 28, 2015 under this project and in collaboration with the Ministry of External Affairs, Government of India where Shri Pinak Ranjan Chakravarty shared his views on India's Look East Policy. The outcome of both the seminars played an important role in shaping this present research work. Field surveys have been conducted in Manipur, Mizoram and Assam to get the ideas of the stakeholders of the region concerning Look East Policy, or the Act East Policy, as we call it today.

This work is divided into five chapters. The first chapter is the introductory chapter outlining the history and development of the Northeastern states from the geostrategic and anthropological point of view. Chapter 1 also gives an idea behind the development of India's Look East Policy and its transformation during the last twenty-five years. The second chapter focuses on the recent trends in the Look East Imagination of India, particularly, the transformation of Look East Policy into Act East Policy. The third chapter is based on the Border field survey particularly at the Moreh-Tamu border, and tries to indentify the opportunities and threats concerning the Border trade of the region. The fourth chapter is mainly focused on Tourism, which is one of the major instruments of connecting the landlocked region of Northeast India with the rest of the world. The final remarks have been summarised in chapter 5 which is the concluding chapter. Moreover, attempts have been made to discuss India-Myanmar relations, India-China relations in different sections of the work.

This project has clearly proved that alongwith physical connectivity, it is important to promote mobility of people as well in the Northeastern Region of India. The conclusion of this work says that the Look East Imagination of India needs and requires a holistic and cross-sectoral approach, which takes into consideration the requirements of physical and soft infrastructure, strengthening connectivity, building entrepreneurial skills, and enhancing sociocultural ties. This multi-sectoral agenda requires participation of several stakeholders, most notably the Northeastern States, the private sector and, most importantly, the people of the Northeastern Region. I am thankful to Dr. Sreeradha Datta, Director, MAKAIAS, for her continued support and patronage to make this project successful. I am also thankful to Professor Om Prakash Mishra, Professor,

Department of International Relations, Jadavpur University, for his continued support and suggestions. I am also thankful to Dr. Suraj L. Singh, who was one of the investigators of this research work. He contributed greatly in forming some of the ideas of the present research. I am also grateful to my student Ms. Sampurna Goswami, Field Assistant, for taking the initiative to conduct field surveys and border visits. I am grateful to Professor Radharaman Chakrabarti, All-India President, JAIR, for his suggestions and advice while writing this project. I am thankful to Monalisa Mohanta, Research Assistant for this project, who has helped me a lot in compiling this present research work. I deeply appreciate the numerous suggestions of my wife, colleagues and friends. Finally, my thanks to Ms Kalpana Shukla and Mr Jose Mathew of KW Publishers Pvt Ltd for publishing this book on time with care and passion.

I am sure that this work will give some inputs to the scholars working in the field of India's Look East Policy and India's Northeastern Region. I am hopeful of conducting a more comprehensive project in the near future on the theme of this research work.

June 30, 2015 **Dr. Imankalyan Lahiri**

Kolkata

ABBREVIATIONS

AEP	Act East Policy
ATTF	All Tripura Tiger Force
AFSPA	Armed Forces Special Powers Act
ADDM	ASEAN Defence Ministers Meeting
ARF	ASEAN Regional Forum
APEC	Asia-Pacific Economic Cooperation
APR	Asia-Pacific Region
AH	Asian Highway
AIIB	Asian Infrastructure Investment Bank
ASIDE	Assistant to States for Infrastructure Development for Exports
ASEAN	Association of South East Asian Nations
BCIM	Bangladesh-China-India-Myanmar
BIMSTEC	Bay of Bengal Initiative for Multi-Sectoral Technical and Economic Cooperation
BLT	Bodo Liberation Tigers
BRICS	Brazil, Russia, India, China and South Africa
BCP	Burma Communist Party
CBEC	Central Board of Excise and Customs
CWC	Central Warehousing Corporation
CII	Confederation of Indian Industry
CARAT	Cooperation Afloat Readiness and Training
DHD	Dima Halam Daogah
DGFT	Director General of Foreign Trade
EAC	East Asian Community
EAS	East Asian Summit
FDI	Foreign Direct Investment
FTA	Free Trade Agreement

GDP	Gross Domestic Product
HRD	Human Resource Development
IIGs	Indian Insurgent Groups
IORARC	Indian Ocean Rim Association for Regional Cooperation
ICP	Integrated Check Post
ISI	Inter-Services Intelligence
IFI	International Financial Institutions
KIA	Kachen Independence Army
KNU	Karen National Union
KI	Kunming Initiative
LCS	Land Customs Stations
LAC	Line of Actual Control
LEP	Look East Policy
MGC	Mekong Ganga Cooperation
MDONER	Ministry of Development of North Eastern Region
MNF	Mizo National Front
NH	National Highway
NLD	National League for Democracy
NLFT	National Liberation Front of Tripura
NSCN	National Socialist Council of Nagaland
NSCN-IM	National Socialist Council of Nagaland-Isak Muivah
NUPA	National Unity Party of Arakan
NGO	Non-Governmental Organisation
NEI	North East India
NEC	North Eastern Council
NER	North Eastern Region
PoK	Pakistan Occupied Kashmir
PPP	Public-Private-Partnership
RCEP	Regional Comprehensive Economic Partnership
RPG	Rocket Propelled Grenades
SAARC	South Asian Association for Regional Cooperation
SAFTA	South Asian Free Trade Agreement

SVP	Stapled Visa Policy
TAH	Trans-Asian Highway
TPP	Trans-Pacific Partnership
TAC	Treaty of Amity and Cooperation
UMFCII	Union of the Myanmar Federation of Chambers of Commerce and Industry
ULFA	United Liberation Front of Asom
UPDS	United People's Democratic Solidarity
UWSA	United Wa State Army

1

LOOK EAST POLICY AND NORTHEAST INDIA: PROSPECTS AND CHALLENGES

Introduction

One of the major features of India's foreign policy today is its "Look East Policy." The Northeastern part of India is the major region of the Indian nation without which it will be difficult for Indian Foreign Policymakers to initiate India's Look East Policy.

Geographically, Northeast India is located in a corner of the Indian nation and has common borders with four neighbouring countries of India: China in the North, Bhutan in the West and Bangladesh and Myanmar in the East and South respectively. No other part of India has such a strategic position as the northeast. Over countless decades, insurgency or militancy as a terrible problem has plagued most parts of Northeast India, and the problem has remained unresolved till today. In many cases the insurgents have multiplied and are still mushrooming, which has resulted in numerous deaths and loss of lives, including those of the rebels, the police, the paramilitary forces as well as innocent lives caught in the crossfire, thereby disturbing normal life in many places in Northeast India. Many indicate that New Delhi is too far off to be even aware of the ground realities, while life in Northeast India is crippled with fear, anxiousness, and uncertainty among common people, the farmers and the traders, with the administration caught in the web of a shadow play. Along with that one of the major developments in the region is that, in 1998, Armed Forces Special Powers Act (AFSPA) was passed by the Government of India in the seven states of Northeast

India, and in Jammu and Kashmir. The Act gives enormous power to the Army Officers who have permissible immunity for their activities. In other words, no prosecution, suit or any other legal proceeding against anyone acting under this law can be broached. So, alternatively, scholars and practitioners are of the opinion that AFSPA allows the Indian Army to terrorise the stakeholders of the states of India where it is operational. As a result AFSPA as a law has given rise to secessionist sentiments in many regions of Northeast India.

Many of the stakeholders in Northeast India believe that it is necessary to abolish AFSPA, so that the people of the region could enjoy democratic rights like other citizens of India. Not only are insurgency and militancy creating disturbances in the region, there are many other events that have been troubling the region for many years. The stakeholders, government, NGOs, students and many other groups are doing their best to establish peace in the region for the last many years. Given the situation that Northeast India is experiencing directly, it is hard to believe that public security, development and community building in Northeast India will be forthcoming in the near future. The Indian government, however, realised the reality and launched its Look East Policy by including Northeast India within the compass of India's Foreign Policy. Initially, the importance of Northeast India as a region was not considered, but with the modification in India's domestic and Foreign Policy, and due to recent developments in the Asian regional order, or rather, due to the rise of *Asian Regionalism*, Indian foreign policymakers want to pay due care to Northeast India, while framing the design for its Look East Policy initiatives. This is more or less evident from the initiatives taken by the Indian government in recent years. However, there are several other problems that exist in the process. It is important for the Indian government to take the people of Northeast India into confidence and some sort of faith must be established towards them. The aim of this project work is to analyse India's Look East Policy in recent years and to link it with India's northeastern region and to find an answer as to whether the Look East Policy could bring peace and development in the Northeastern Region of India in real conditions. This will be followed by an analysis of how India's Look East Policy could help in the community development process in northeastern India.

The new geopolitical ideas developed by contemporary strategic thinkers working in the field of present research and developing the framework of innovative policy understanding, developed an area that simply refuses to remain confined by the present geography of Northeast India and wishes to sway to the countries of Southeast Asia, Asia-Pacific and South Asia through such frontier states as Myanmar, China and Bangladesh by crossing the international borders. The whole of the Northeast as formally conceived now has therefore a significant effect in the field of present research, and also provides a significant influence to the alternative models of imagining the Northeast in the contemporary understanding of India's domestic and International policies. It is to be noted here that Northeast India is the geographical space between two subregions of Asia, namely, South Asia and Southeast Asia. Both these regions are in the process of change, set off by economic rise and the process of evolution. However, for many reasons, we in India have failed to attract the various opportunities that this subregion of India has to offer towards the welfare and the well-being of the people. It is significant again to understand the region, not merely as the geographical component of being a bridgehead between South Asia and Southeast Asia, but also as the storehouse of natural and human resources. Today, the challenge is to grasp these opportunities to make certain that growth and development do not ignore this region, but involve the region at large.

Situating the Northeastern Region of India

Historically, the geopolitical segregation of the northeastern region took place during the partition of India in 1947. Undoubtedly, the partition created chaos and that chaos had a negative impact on the development of the Northeast. It made the Northeast the most controlled and susceptible border region, and the most exposed territory. The partition caused the closing of the inland water and railway communications in the region through what is now Bangladesh (East Pakistan, after partition). For example, the access to the Chittagong seaport was lost after the separation of India, which created several problems for Northeast India. Calcutta (now Kolkata) became the nearest port, several hundred kilometres away from the region. Agartala, which was only 350 kilometres from Calcutta through Dacca (now Dhaka), shifted to nearly 1,600 kilometres away. Moreover, Chinese occupation of Tibet and the blockage of the border of India with Burma added more isolation of the area. This blockage shattered this region economically.[1]

On the positive side, people from different sectors have talked about economic integration of the northeastern states with mainland India for several decades after partition. For many years, policymakers, bureaucrats and intellectuals have tried to stop the numerous armed separatist struggles that caused political instability in the northeastern states. They concentrated on improving the region's underdeveloped and weak economic condition and felt the urgency to integrate Northeast India with mainland India to work out these troubles and to establish peace in the region. As a component of this attempt to incorporate the region with the rest of India, the government of India started to sanction sufficient funds and emphasis was laid on the growth and infrastructural development in the area. Despite this, the region is still severely underdeveloped and still lives under threat and suspicion. Illegal migrants from Bangladesh, Nepal and Myanmar have added tensions in the area. Altogether, these factors are creating unrest in the area and such unrest has resulted in anxiety, which threatens the protection of the region by hindering the progress and development of a strategically significant part of India. Moreover, the entire neighbourhood of Northeast India is poor in industrial development, and there is no specific industrial policy both on the part of the government and the individual investors in the region, which leads to the increase in the costs of transportation of goods. Major industrial groups are also apathetic toward investment in the region, even though many of them are very much operative in the region in terms of research and observation. Thus, the existing policies of development of the northeastern region needed to be reshaped if the stated objectives have to be met in the years to come.[2]

It is known to all of us that the defining feature of India is "Unity in Diversity." It is comfortably known to us that each and every part of India respects this attribute along with a strong underlying sense of national unity and *Indianness* at the centre of this diversity. Also, a former Minister of State of Indian Union Ministry of External Affairs once defined the multicultural feature of India as "Diversity in Unity."[3] This rich mixture of diversity can be more significantly observed in the northeastern provinces of India. It is important to note here that Northeast India is naturally rich in resources and nature has presented this entire region abundantly in many respects. To mention a few, the region has a rich biodiversity; unparalleled potential to develop hydro-energy, has reserves of petroleum and natural gas, is rich in minerals and likewise has huge timber resources. But, more importantly, it is the people of the area, which is a unique endowment, being a consequence of the merging of diverse cultural, lingual, spiritual, ethnic and educational patterns.[4] It is now time to cultivate the human resources of Northeast India along with the other natural resources. It is necessary to generate the idea amongst the people of the northeastern region that they form an integral part of India and their role in defining India's feature of "Unity in Diversity" is important since India's rise in the age of globalisation would be incomplete without their participation and cooperation.

In spite of having tremendous natural and human resources, as pointed out earlier, the region is largely underdeveloped. The process of industrialisation was initiated in this area by the East India Company under the British rule in the early nineteenth century with the nurturing and the first export of tea way back in 1839, but the speedy increase of manufacture has not taken place. Though coal was found here, it was destroyed by the colonial rulers. Coal was primarily used for the running of the railroad. During this time the policy of coal preservation was not followed. In the year 1901, the first oil refinery in Asia was set up in Digboi following the discovery of oil in Upper Assam. Along with oil, tea and jute industries started to grow to some extent. It is significant to recall that during times of severe foreign exchange crisis in the past, Assam's tea and jute exports remained one of the major sources of earning foreign exchange. It is all the more ironic and disheartening that today this region is yet to derive full benefit from the industrialisation and economic evolution of our nation, and that significant conflicts are evident in terms of development indicators compared to other regions of India. For example, if we take the case study of Assam we will get the real picture of the situation. Assam is often described as a *land of poverty in the midst of plenty*, it is also described as a region of neglected potentialities and unrealised opportunities. There are vast resources of minerals, oil, natural gas, coal, limestone, forests, and water resources holding out prospects of rapid industrialisation in Assam. In spite of this, Assam happens to be one of the most backward states in India in terms of industrial development. Major industries in the Indian public sector are mostly built by the Government of India. Private enterprises and the Union government have shown no interest in the industrialisation of Assam, instead coveting its raw material. The Union government has made about twenty per cent of its investment in Maharashtra and Gujerat as compared to only five per cent in this region. There are many factors for the underdevelopment of Assam. Industrialisation is handicapped mainly by Assam's isolation from the rest of India along with a poor transportation system, small local markets, the lack of sufficient capital and entrepreneurs, the structural weakness of Assam's economy, the Government of India's reluctance in licensing industries in Assam, and finally, the non-Assamese control of its trade, commerce and industry.[5] It may be mentioned here that tea is the main agricultural product in Assam. Before Assam's reorganisation in 1972, there were seven hundred fifty-two tea gardens, while the number now is nearly nine hundred. Assam today is producing nearly sixty per cent of the country's tea. Assam's tea is earning huge foreign exchange, but, surprisingly, the financial benefits go to non-Assamese people. This is so for several reasons. First, these tea estates are not owned by the Assamese. Secondly, the bulk of tea output is sold and distributed in Kolkata by a system of auctions that bring no substantial benefit to the state. Since the major portion of Assam tea is marketed not at the Guwahati Auction Centre but at the Kolkata Centre, it is the West Bengal government that receives most of the revenue by way of sales tax on Assam produced tea. The royalties received by West Bengal from the Government of India for Assamese tea are more than what is received by Assam. Moreover, the head offices of the tea industry, such as the Indian Tea Association, are located in Kolkata, thus providing job opportunities to the people of West Bengal. On the other hand, Assam also produces about forty per cent of India's jute, but has only one jute mill in the cooperative sector, which is The Assam Cooperative Jute Mills Ltd. which is located at Silghat, in the Nagaon district of Assam. This jute mill was registered in the year 1959 under the Assam Cooperative Societies Act. It is impossible to process all the raw jute by this single mill, so almost all the raw jute goes to feed the mills in Kolkata.[6] There are, however, some private jute mills in Assam, but their potential output is negligible.

Similar problems remain for all the other states of Northeast India. There is a widening gap between the rich and the poor in many of the states. Connectivity in the region is poor and so it is unmanageable for any industry to grow. Sometimes connectivity between the urban fields and the rural areas of the region is lost. It is also true that, since independence, Indian business houses have ignored the region greatly and have not initiated any major industry plan, as pointed out earlier.

Today, the Northeast is in the process of reviving the past. The global emerging market economy has created a consciousness among the stakeholders in the area. In the normal course, it is anticipated that the consciousness would soon take a proper shape. Indian business talent would find newer dimensions in the region. As discussed above, there was a time when mainland entrepreneurs were not very welcome in these uninitiated lands. The reasons were many, and they will be discussed in due course. Even so, that posture is shifting in recent years. New articipation from different sectors is taking different directions. At the same time it is anticipated that with the process of investment "the region's geopolitical isolation" may be broken and then neutralised. Nevertheless, the question remains: how far could the local economic system cope with equal and sustainable purchasing power and supply the necessary human resources for such developmental operations which might grow in the age of globalisation? The result would decide the destiny of the entire region. On the other hand, if the cognitive operation of investment demands a good shape in the region, it has to be created on a positive approach. There have to be inputs from diverse but interrelated fields, including defence, foreign insurance, national security and foreign craft which have to be absorbed carefully. The substantial positive sign is that a foundation has been built and the Government of India is seriously thinking of this. This is clear from the different initiatives that the government has adopted in recent years.

There has been growing realisation by the Indian leaders and bureaucrats that development of physical connectivity with Southeast Asia (and also with Asia-Pacific Region) is an important condition to fully utilise the opportunities intended to be offered by India's Look East Policy. In the initiatives to frame the Look East Policy relevant for the region, India has placed greater stress on enhancing connectivity through all the potential modes of infrastructure development, such as land, air and water routes, energy infrastructure development both in the study of hydroelectric, hydrocarbon and telecommunication linkages. As a consequence, India has initiated some bilateral projects and multilateral projects, aimed at increasing the connectivity between the Northeast, Southeast Asia and the Asia-Pacific region. Nevertheless, within the existing possibilities the process of enhancing connectivity between India's Northeast and Southeast Asia (including Asia-Pacific region) is not an easy task because there are also geographical, technological, political and security challenges that will affect the practical operation of this growth. These challenges are manageable. What is needed now is to initiate intra-regional capacity building plans in the Northeast, which will include the development of better connectivity within the region, development of basic and export oriented industries, development of technical and entrepreneurial accomplishments in the local population through different training programmes, and finally to arrive at a consensus on a common agenda for the development of the Northeast, to utilise all the approved funds sanctioned for its development by the government and the international agencies in an effective and result-oriented way. To do this, at the micro-level, corruption in any form in the different states of the Northeast has to be reduced and more awareness has to be created. People living in the periphery of different areas of the Northeast have to be linked with the people who are aware of the developmental projects initiated by the Government for the northeastern region. The political leaders of the region must quickly adapt themselves to the development projects and influence others to adopt it. Similarly, at the macro-level, the Northeast should be directly included in various subregional initiatives, such as the The Bay of Bengal Initiative for Multi-Sectoral Technical and Economic Cooperation (BIMSTEC), Mekong Ganga Cooperation and Kunming initiative, as a separate economic entity, which, in turn, would facilitate the harnessing of available regional economic opportunities. The bottom line is that the idea of enhancing connectivity between the Northeast and Southeast Asia is a very important step and holds the potential to change the social and economic landscape of the region. The aim is not only to create this effective atmosphere for the region to grow but also to recognise that it should be supplemented by efforts to keep the region ready for any type of investments.[7]

With the paradigm switch from a state-centred approach to one of interdependence and global and regional cooperation, we have become all the more aware of the geo-economic potential of the northeastern region as an entryway to East Asia and Southeast Asia. It is a fact that by steadily integrating this region through cross-border market access, the northeastern states can establish the link between the Indian economy and what is arguably the fastest developing and most vibrant area in the world. But, before we progress further, it is important for us to examine the present condition of Northeast India, which is creating a barrier towards the proper implementation of India's Look East Policy through the region itself, the economic aspects of which have been identified. The region today is in the midst of insurgency, anti-state activities, repression and instability. In many cases the logic of the local inhabitants of the region is different from that of the framers of India's Look East Policy. Therefore, it is significant for us to identify the basic problem of the region, that which is acting as a roadblock in the way of implementing India's Look East Policy. This project endeavours to give a background of the existing political and societal instability that exists in the region and concentrate on some of the aspects of how to get rid of the present crises. To explain this, relevant historical contexts will be mentioned in this chapter. It is evident that without analysing the root cause of the problems in Northeast India, India's Look East Policy cannot be worked. In other words, peace and stability in Northeast India are a required condition to implement it.

Northeast India: The Population

India's northeast is comprised of the state of Sikkim[8] and the other seven states of India, namely, Assam, Arunachal Pradesh,[9] Manipur,[10] Meghalaya,[11] Mizoram,[12] Nagaland[13] and Tripura.[14] The northeastern region is surrounded by countries like Bhutan, China, Burma, and Bangladesh on the North-South and the East except for a long, narrow passageway in the West which connects the region with West Bengal and the rest of India. It is estimated that these States cover a total area of over 255,088 sq. km (7.7 per cent of the country's territory) and, according to the 2011 Census of India, a population of 45,486,784 persons (3.76 per cent of national population). Table 1 gives the idea of the State-wise distribution of Population in India's Northeastern Region.

Table 1: State-wise Distribution of Population (Census 2011, Government of India) *

States	Population			Rural			Urban		
	Total	Male	Female	Total	Male	Female	Total	Male	Female
Arunachal Pradesh	1383727	713912	669815	1066358	546011	520347	317369	167901	149468
Assam	31205576	15939443	15266133	26807034	13678989	13128045	4398542	2260454	2138088
Manipur	2570390	1290171	1280219	1736236	878469	857767	834154	411702	422452
Meghalaya	2966889	1491832	1475057	2371439	1194260	1177179	595450	297572	297878
Mizoram	1097206	555339	541867	525435	269135	256300	571771	286204	285567
Nagaland	1978502	1024649	953853	1407536	725472	682064	570966	299177	271789
Sikkim	610577	323070	287507	456999	242797	214202	153578	80273	73305
Tripura	3673917	1874376	1799541	2712464	1387173	1325291	961453	487203	474250
Total NER	45486784	23212792	22273992	37083501	18922306	18161195	8403283	4290486	4112797

* Table 1 be may be represented graphically as in Figure 1.

Figure 1: Gender-wise Population of Northeastern States

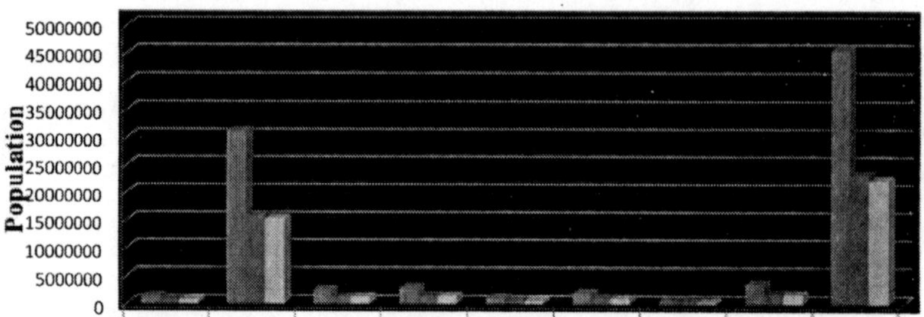

	Arunachal Pradesh	Assam	Manipur	Meghalaya	Mizoram	Nagaland	Sikkim	Tripura	Total NER
Total	1383727	31205576	2570390	2966889	1097206	1978502	610577	3673917	45486784
Male	713912	15939443	1290171	1491832	555339	1024649	323070	1874376	23212792
Female	669815	15266133	1280219	1475057	541867	953853	287507	1799541	22273992

The population of Northeast India is the mixture of a large number of cultural groups who migrated from different directions at various historical times. These groups are comprised of various racial identities having diverse social and ethnic customs and speaking different languages. For most of them, Northeast India is their indigenous soil. This area has been occupied by different streams of the *Mongoloid* people who came from the north and the east of the region at different phases of history. Scholars are of the view that the *Australoids* group of human population came to this area prior to the coming of the *Mongoloids*, who partially or fully absorbed the Australoid strains. In other words, the physical characteristics of different kin groups of Northeast India suggest that the *Australoid* elements are present in some form or the other in different groups of people who migrated to the region in the past. It has been stated historically that long ago one segment of the *Indo-Mongoloids* population spread over the whole of the Brahmaputra valley, North Bengal and East Bengal (now Bangladesh) giving rise to various tribal groups inhabiting this region (Chaterji, 1974: 27-28). The diverse *Mongoloid* groups steadily settled down in different habitats and ecological settings of the northeastern region and condensed into distinct entities which are referred to as *tribes* of the region today. This is important to note that the migration of people from ancient to present times and from various directions to Northeast India have extensively contributed towards the growth of ethnic diversities in the region. Besides the tribal groups, a few other non-tribal groups have also come into existence as a consequence of prolonged interaction between the cultures of the migrants and those of the indigenous people. The spread of Hinduism and other sects of Hinduism including *Vaishnavism*; invasions of different outside rulers at different historical periods; integration of the northeastern region with the rest of India in the nineteenth century and migrations that took place as late as the last century have also greatly transformed the region socially, culturally, economically and politically.[15]

Ethnic Problems in Northeastern Region: An Overview

One of the important dimensions of politics of the springing up world that affects the domestic and the International politics is the ethnic struggles and conflict resolution. Ethnic conflict refers to the fight that takes place between two or more "ethnic communities." According to Anthony Smith (1993), an "ethnic community" is "a named human population with a myth of common ancestry, shared memories, and cultural elements; a link with a historic territory or homeland; and a measure of solidarity." Michael E. Brown's *Ethnic Conflict and International Security* (1993) is an excellent book that deals with the impact of ethnic conflict on International Politics. He considers, even though some systematic conditions are essential for ethnic conflict to occur, it is collective memory that forms the preconditions of the conflict. The structural factors he identifies in the ethnic conflict are: *First*, more than one ethnic group must live in close proximity; *secondly*, national, regional and international authorities must not be very strong to prevent groups from fighting and too weak to ensure the protection of private groups. The refugee problem and the use of weapons is the natural result of the ethnic conflict, Brown noted. But, interestingly enough, the ethnic problem in Northeast has its own peculiar features which may be different from the idea of the ethnic problem as conceived by Smith or Brown. Today, the Northeast India is marked by amazing ethnic, cultural, religious and linguistic diversity, with more than 160 Scheduled Tribes belonging to five different ethnic groups, and a large and diverse non-tribal population as well.[16] There are three widely accepted terminologies of the group of people referred to as Scheduled Tribes in the Indian context. These are: (a) *Tribals,* (b) *Adivasis* and (c) *Indigenous People.* Scholars have pointed out that it is difficult to identify as well as to define tribes. Scholars have also pointed out that there has been more anxiety with the identification of *tribes* than with their definition. However, there are several measures used to identify and define *tribes* which range from such features as geographical seclusion, primitive technology, condition of living, a general backwardness to the practice of animism, tribal language, physical characteristics, and many others. The problem, however, lay in the fact that due to the limited knowledge and involvement of the scholars, the geographical location, origin of their languages, their knowledge towards science and technology, etc., have not been clearly formulated nor scientifically applied while identifying and defining the tribes. Thus, their identification creates a great problem for the scholars who deal with them. It may be noted here that tribes in the central, western and southern part of India prefer to call themselves *Adivasis* rather than tribes. The term *Adivasi,* however, has little acceptance amongst the population in the northeastern region of the country with the term generally being used by them to refer to that group of people who work in the tea gardens in Assam. Scholars are of the opinion that the term "Adivasi," therefore, is used in the East and Northeast India for identifying the migrant tribal labourers and small peasants of Central India. As a result the local populations in these States find it humiliating to identify themselves as *Adivasi.* On the other hand, the concept of the tribe has been conceptualised and theorised by various scholars who define tribes as "nationalities." Simply that many scholars do not concur with this and prefer to call the *clans* as an *ethnic* group. According to many scholars *tribes* are the targets of various categorisation processes. From the position of the "others," they name themselves as Primitive Society, Tribe,

Segmented Society, Aborigines, Backward Hindus, ethnic minority, Nation and Nationalities, primitive to post-primitive, vulnerable, culturo-political entities, *adivasis*, or indigenous people.[17] It is noteworthy that the tribal communities in Northeast India are living along the boundary of three great political communities: India, China and Burma (Myanmar). Historically, some of them took active roles in the process of integration of various communities. For example, in the pre-colonial times of the region, especially in the Khasi and Jaintia regions, Kachari and Chutiya kingdoms, ethnicity was a determining component in the organisation of society over and above other factors that were relevant at that time in regard to the formation of societies.

With the passage of time external powers started to influence the lives of the tribal population in Northeast India. The situation started to change when help was extended by East India Company to the *Ahom* Kingdom to stop the Burmese invasion and the *Treaty of Yandaboo* was signed,[18] by which the Ahom King surrendered a portion of his land to the British East India Company as a reward in the year 1826. Thereafter the British continuously expanded their administration in the area. It may be pointed out here that Assam was part of the Bengal Province of British India until 1874. Nevertheless, there was a restructuring of the region under the colonial rulers. As a result, the two princely states of Manipur and Tripura came under the British command after the British conquest in 1891. The history of Northeast India until India's independence was a story of the expansion of British regulation and of social, economic and political changes in the neighbourhood. However, during the initial years of colonial rule, the British avoided interfering in the activities of the tribal population. Scholars are of the belief that the British Government was tending, on the whole, to leave the tribesmen alone, largely because the responsibility of governance, particularly in the border areas, was difficult and the areas unreachable.

Gradually, the British rulers in India initiated an innovative policy to rule the tribal people living in the hill areas. They developed a policy which may be termed as the *policy of non-interference* and it was particularly applicable to the hill communities, especially in the northeastern region of India. Moreover, the *policy of non-interference* was followed to restrict opposition from the hill communities to the colonial rulers who were very much interested to pursue their commercial activities in the region. This policy was initiated because the tribal communities in the hill areas of the northeastern region initially objected greatly to British activities in their neighbourhood. The other reason for the implementation of this policy was that it was too hard for the colonial rulers to control the region because of the differences in language and cultural mindset. Thus the policy of non-interference initially made the tribal people apathetic towards the British rulers. With the passage of time, tribal communities who predominantly inhabited the hills areas were forcefully merged with the princely states and into different districts for the so-called "administrative convenience" of the colonial rulers. In due course the hill communities in Northeast India were taken under different territorial administrative authorities and thus the concept of territorial politics was introduced, hitherto unknown to the hill communities. This is possibly the root cause of the troubles we are confronting in the northeastern region today. But the data we get about the region today is essentially based on the mapping of the tribes in the region by the ethnographers of the colonial times. It was difficult for Indian ethnographers to conduct research in those areas at that time due to several reasons. As a result the colonial ethnographers became the pioneers in documenting the tribes in the northeast. Thus, we cannot undermine their contribution in terms of knowledge and data along the northeastern region, particularly on tribes. However, their methodology and motive may be problematic.[19] Today, there are several scholars who are doing their best to determine the basic cause of the troubles in the northeastern part of India. Most of them will agree upon the fact that the problems in the Northeast had a radical orientation during the colonial times and assumed various shapes and builds in later years varying from anti-state activities to inter-tribal differences. Today, this problem is still persisting in Northeast India. Inter-tribe disputes still exist in the region. Many new factors have been added to this. There is also a rise of Scheduled Tribe population during the last several years. Their numbers today are noteworthy. Table 2 gives us an estimate of the distribution of the Scheduled Tribe Population in the Northeastern Region of India in recent years:

Table 2: Tribal Population in the Northeastern Region[20]

State	Total Population	ST Population	Percentage of ST
Arunachal Pradesh	1383727	951821	68.79
Assam	31205576	3884371	12.45
Manipur	2570390	902740	35.12
Meghalaya	2966889	2555861	86.15
Mizoram	1097206	1036115	94.43
Nagaland	1978502	1710973	86.48
Sikkim	610577	206360	33.80
Tripura	3673917	1166813	31.76
Total NER	45486784	12415054	27.29

The Tribal population of the Northeastern Region may be represented as below:

Figure 2: Scheduled Tribe Population in Northeastern Region Government (Census 2011, Government of India)

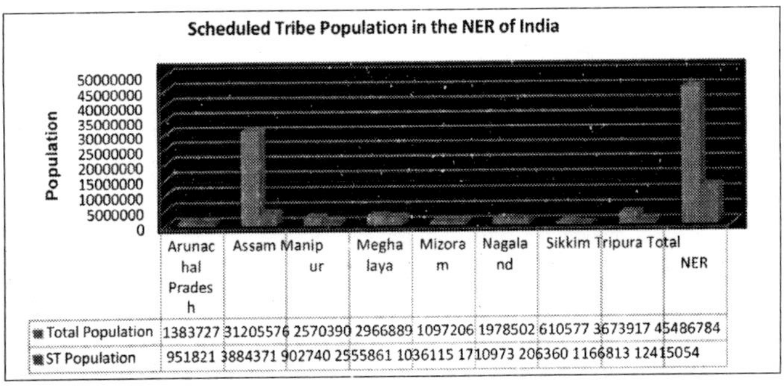

Today, Northeast India comprises very many tribal groups with distinct characteristics. Table 3 gives us an idea of the major tribal groups in the different Northeastern States as it is today.

Table 3: State-wise List of Tribes in Northeast India

Arunachal Pradesh	Assam	Meghalaya
Abor	In the autonomous	Chakma
Aka	Districts of Karbi	Dimasa, Kachari
Apatani	Anglong and North Cachar	Garo
Nyishi	Hills:	Hajong
Galo	Hmar	
Khampti	Chakma	Khasi, Jaintia, Synteng, Pnar,
Khowa	Dimasa, Kachari	War, Bhoi,
Mishmi, Idu,	Garo	Lyngngam
Taroan	Hajong	Lakher
Momba	Hmar	Mạn (Tai Speaking)
Any Naga tribes	Khasi:	Any Mizo (Lushai) tribes
Sherdukpen	Jaintia	Mikir
Singpho	Synteng	Any Naga tribes
Hrusso	Pnar,	Pawi
Tagin	War	Synteng
Khamba	Bhoi,	Boro Kacharis
Adi	Lyngngam	Koch
Manipur	Any Kuki tribes,	Raba, Rava
Aimol	including:	Any Kuki tribes, including:
Anal	Biate, Biete	Biate, Biete
Angami	Changsan	Changsan
Chiru	Chongloi	Chongloi
Chothe	Doungel	Doungel
Gangte	Gamalhou	Gamalhou
Hmar	Gangte	Gangte
Kabui, Inpui,Rongmei	Guite	Guite
Kacha,Naga,	Hanneng	Hanneng
Liangmai, Zeme		
Koirao,Thangal	Haokip, Haupit	Haokip, Haupit
Koireng	Haolai	Haolai xi. Hengna
Kom	Hengna	Hongsungh
Lamgang	Hongsungn	Hrangkhwal, Rangkhol
Mao	Hrangkhwal,	Jongbe
Maram	Rangkhol	Khawchung

Maring	Jongbe	Khawathlang,
Any Mizo (Lushai)	Khawchung	Khothalong
tribes	Khawathlang	Khelma
Monsang	Khothalong	Kholhou
Moyon	Khelma	Kipgen
Paite	Kholhou	Kuki
Purum	Kipgen	Lengthang
Ralte	Kuki	Lhangum
Sema	Lengthang	Lhoujem
Simte	Lhangum	Lhouvun
Suhte	Lhoujem	Lupheng
Tangkhul	Lhouvun	Mangjel
Thadou	Lupheng	Misao
Vaiphui	Mangjel	Riang
Zou	Misao	Sairhem
Poumai Naga	Riang	Selnam
Tarao	Sairhem	Singson
Kharam	Selnam	Sitlhou
Any Kuki tribes	Singson	Sukte
Mate	Sitlhou	Thado
Mizoram	Sukte	Thangngeu
Chakma	Thado	Uibuh
Dimasa (Kachari)	Thangngeu	Vaiphei
Garo	Uibuh	**Nagaland**
Hajong	Vaiphei	Naga
Hmar	Lakher	Kuki
Khasi and Jaintia,	Man (Tai speaking)	Kachari
(Including Khasi,	Any Miz (Lushai) tribes	Mikir
Synteng or Pnar, War,	Karbi	Garo
Bhoi or Lyngngam)		Paite
Lakher	Any Naga tribes	**Sikkim**
Man (Tai-speaking)	Pawi	Bhutia (including Chumbipa,
Any Mizo (Lushai)	Syntheng	Dopthap, Dukpa, Kagatey,
tribes		Sherpa, Tibetan, Tromop,
Mikir	Lalung	Yolmo)
Any Naga tribes.		Lepcha
Pawi	II. In the State of	Limboo
Synteng	Assam including the	
Any Kuki Tribes,	Bodo land territorial	
including Biate, Biete	Areas District and	
Changsan	excluding the	
Chongloi	autonomous districts	
	of Karbi Anglong and	
	North Cachar Hills	

Doungel		Tamang
Gamalhou		**Tripura**
Gangte		Bhil
Guite	1. Barmans in Cachar	Bhutia
Hanneng	2. Boro, Borokachari	Chaimal
Haokip, Haupit	3. Deori	Chakma
Haolai xi. Hengna	4. Hojai	Garoo
Hongsungh	5. Kachari, Sonwal	Halam, *Bengshel, Dub,*
Hrangkhwal,	6. Lalung	Kaipeng, Kalai, Karbong,
Rangkhol	7. Mech	Lengui, Mussum, Rupini,
Jongbe	8. Miri	Sukuchep, Thangchep
Khawchung	9. Rabha	Jamatia
Khawathlang,	10. Dimasa	Khasia
Khothalong	11. Hajong	Lepcha
Khelma	12. Singhpho	Lushai
Kholhou	13. Khampti	Mag
Kipgen	14. Garo	Munda,Kaur
Kuki		Noatia, Murashing
Lengthang		Orang
Lhangum		Riang
Lhoujem		Santal
Lhouvun		Tripura, Tripuri, Tippera
Lupheng		Uchai
Mangjel		Kuki, including:
Misao		the following sub-tribes: (i)
Riang		Balte (ii) Belalhut
Sairhem		(iii) Chhalya (iv) Fun
Selnam		(v) Hajango
Singson		(vi) Jangtei (vii) Khareng
Sitlhou		(viii) Khephong (ix) Kuntei
Sukte		(x) Laifang (xi) Lentei
Thado		(xii) Mizel (xiii) Namte
Thangngeu		(xiv) Paitu, Paite
Uibuh		(xv) Rangchan (xvi)
Vaiphei		Rangkhole (xvii) Thangluya

As pointed out earlier, the political culture of Northeast India today is marked by ethnicity and extremism for a long time. The assertion of various ethnic identities and the attitude of the state in containing ethnic extremism made the region distinct from the rest of India. The original cause of ethnic unrest can be found in the identity crisis of various tribal communities who extend beyond the territorial boundaries created by the Indian state. Most of the ethnic crises we are facing today in the region are due to ethnic groups' aggressive attempts to protect their identity, culture and language. For example, it is argued that *claims to ethno-nationalism of the Bodos can be interpreted as closely intertwined with issues of institutional and social exclusion based on language politics* (Saikia, 2011: 60). In other words, the basis of ethnic assertion can be seen in two contexts. *First,* there is always a subjective consciousness amongst the tribals of being excluded, oppressed and marginalised. The history of the region has proved this idea. The colonial rulers as well as the post-colonial rulers never concentrated on this issue very much. *Secondly,* the process of development failed to address the legitimate rights of the people of this region. It may be mentioned here that when the Ahom Kingdom of Assam was weakened, rebellion broke out and gradually the whole land witnessed confusion and misery. In like manner of the Ahoms, the Chin-Lushai-Kukis had faced the same problem. The colonial rulers isolated the land by implementing the Inner Line Regulations called, *The Bengal, Eastern Frontier Regulation, 1973 (Regulation V of 1873) amended in 1873.* As a result, the inner line passes were introduced. The passes were required for the *Lushais* to enter into British India. The Inner Line Regulation was practised on the reverse from 1925. Since then *non-Lushais* were not allowed to enter in the *Lushai*[21] country without passes duly signed by designated or authorised officers. It was revealed that the *Lushais* being external people were regarded as foreigners by the British. The Nagas and the North Cachar people also fell in the same category.[22] This isolation is continuing till date. Today Indian citizens too need to have inner line permits to enter into the states of Manipur, Mizoram, Arunachal Pradesh and Nagaland. Foreigners also need to have requisite permits to enter into many of the regions of Northeast India.

Though after independence the Indian state tried to amalgamate and assimilate various ethnic communities in the mainstream national identity, the development process generated a feeling of disaffection among them. Moreover, development led to the unequal distribution of resources across the population of the region. Hence, the cultural, political as well as economic factors created a sense of exclusion among some ethnic communities. This is also clear from the writing of Upa K. Saibela in 1997 which states, in Mizo language: "India Independent tirh atanga kum 50-na inkarahian, kan khawtlang nunah na na na hi chuan, a tha lam aiin a chhe lamah thil a danglam a ni tih kan hre theuhvin ka ring,"[23] which means, in English, that during the fifty years of independence, things have gone astray in the wrong directions in respect of our social life, in particular.

In Northeast India, the fear of exclusion started even before Independence. Since the colonial times there was a fear amongst the indigenous population that they might lose their right to land, territories and resources which they have traditionally owned. The *Nagas* predicted the chance of elimination in post-colonial India in the case of their integration with the Indian Union, and started mobilising Nagas for a separate nation free from the domination of the Indian nation. Moreover, they also felt that their community life and values would be threatened with the increasing number of different communities from other parts of India. It is pertinent to say that the Nagas, who were politically and culturally one of the active ethnic minorities, demanded separation from India as soon as India became independent. From 1956 onwards, the movement became violent in nature and the groups started to use violence as a means to achieve their goals. By the mid of the 1960s, the Nagas joined the Mizos. Despite several decades of low-level insurgency, neither group could achieve their demand for separation. Details have been discussed in the later part of this chapter. The sense of this social exclusion in the Northeast was articulated with the emergence of new social forces—educated elite (many of them got an appointment in the government sector), students, youth groups and others. It is again important to note here that the diffusion among the local population started due to the weak ties between the ethnic groups, on the one side, and the government and the local population, on the other. Since the demand for identity is the demand of the disconnected groups of Northeast India, it created political diffusion and led to the emergence of new social forces creating a gap in the network of the groups. Other reasons for the emergence of social forces in the Northeast include, the emergence of Christianity and its impact on the sociocultural and economic life of the people, spread of education, etc. These factors acted as major agents of recent changes in the northeastern region. In other words, the emergence of a market-economy in India also brought a change in the northeastern region in recent times. All these factors together contributed greatly in this change. More specifically, scholars have identified three major agents of change among the tribes of Northeast India. These are (a) *the state* (b) *civil society*, the Church remained a major force behind the emergence of civil society and (c) *market forces*. (Oommen, 2009: 10). At the same time, ethnic identity provided the ground for the mobilisation of ethnic groups. It is argued that the process of ethnic identity formation in the northeastern region was based largely on the idea of *group* formation (Karna, 1991). They were able to form groups because of technological mobility and the rise of modern communication systems. Moreover, the social exclusion of ethnic communities has a dialectical link with psychological exclusion of the tribal communities of the region. These include exclusion from formal governmental and non-governmental institutions. The tribals think that this exclusion is due to their lack of cognitive orientation and the epistemological inequality due to lack of access to epistemological resources. The impersonation of their social, cultural, economic and political life with people from other communities or modern states further accelerated this process.[24]

In this backdrop, we have to review the fact that India's Northeast has been the land of many insurgencies. The emotional power of appeals of ethnicity has created a new momentum in the present-day world order characterised by the forces of globalisation and the shrinking of national boundaries. Demands by ethnic groups in several countries for secession from the wider state system have become an important feature of political development. Similarly, India has problems with several regions of the country which threaten the integrity of the nation. Many troubles have gone up in the course of the origination of a greater Indian consciousness, which has been the goal of the Government in New Delhi, and which has yet to be reached. While the idea has been that the greater Indian consciousness would submerge the consciousness of smaller nationalities, the trend in India seems to have been the other fashion. Northeast India is one such region, which is preventing India from producing a greater Indian Consciousness.[25] Alternatively, the ethnic struggle in Northeast India has given rise to insurgency since 1947. Starting with the *Naga* insurgency since India's independence in 1947, several insurgency movements have sprung up in most of the states of the region. There was a time when about 120 insurgent groups spread their activities in the seven states of the Northeast, excluding Sikkim (Sikkim was bracketed under Northeast in 2003). Interestingly enough, the demands of the insurgent groups have been wide-ranging. Groups like the *United Liberation Front of Asom* (ULFA) and *National Socialist Council of Nagaland: Isak-Muivah* (NSCN-IM) aim at establishing independent states. On the other hand, armed Bodo tribesmen wanted their own "Bodoland" state which they can themselves rule. Groups like Bodo Liberation Tigers (BLT) demanded separate states for their tribal constituency. Other organisations, such as the *United People's Democratic Solidarity* (UPDS) and *Dima Halam Daogah* (DHD), confining their activities to some districts in Assam, have fought for maximum autonomy within the purview of the Indian constitution. The reasons behind dissent against the Indian state are many. The *National Liberation Front of Tripura* (NLFT) and the *All Tripura Tiger Force* (ATTF) insurgencies in Tripura are rooted in the sense of alienation of the indigenous tribes due to the constant migration from Bangladesh (formerly East

Pakistan). One of the agendas of ULFA was to highlight the problems Assam is facing as a result of Bangladeshi migration. On the other hand, in Manipur, several groups operated in the valley areas of Manipur to protest against the forcible accession of the state to the Indian union and subsequent neglect of their language and the delayed statehood conferred on the state. Similarly, apathy shown by the central government to the area suffering from a famine triggered the militancy in Mizoram spearheaded by the *Mizo National Front* (MNF).[26]

Thus, it is to be accepted that the India's Independence developed some sort of anxiety amongst the tribal population of the region. In many cases the Government of India has failed to address the micro-level problem that exists in the region. The Look East Policy initiated by the Government of India is undoubtedly a tool to remove the problem of isolation in Northeast India, but there is the *lack of trust* that the Indian government has failed to address. The involvement of the common stakeholders of Northeast India is necessary for the proper execution of India's Look East policy without which the problems in the northeastern region cannot be worked out. Therefore fear of isolation is likely to continue. However, India has been successful in integrating ethnic diversities because it eventually bowed to popular demands for "linguistic" and "tribal" ethnic states. India's ethnic diversity is not a problem to be fully solved, but one that is to be managed continuously.

Northeast India: The Problems of the Region

It is known to everyone today that India's Northeast is the region of the earliest and longest lasting insurgency in the country. The problem of insurgency started in Nagaland in 1952, and gradually multiplicity of more recent fights have proliferated, especially since the late 1970s. Most of the states in the Northeastern Region today witness scales of conflict that can be categorised as low-intensity wars, and may be defined as conflicts in which fatalities are more than normal every year.

Historically speaking, and as already noted, Northeast India is a creation of the Partition of India. Before partition, there was no concept of a separate northeast region, and that was the time when all the provinces or hill regions that now constitute the northeastern region were closely linked. Also, trade, economy, movement and education, to the adjoining areas of East Bengal or Burma (today's Myanmar) was a common feature at that time. For example, the *Khasi, Jaintia* and *Garo* Hills maintained close relations with *Sylhet*, the Mizo hills with the Chittagong Hills Tracts and Tripura with *Comilla, Noakhali* and *Sylhet.* During this time, parts of the Mizo Hills, Manipur and the Naga Hills had direct links with Burma, where many of their ethnic kinsmen lived. The areas of the former North-East Frontier Agency (now Arunachal Pradesh) had close contacts with Tibet and Bhutan. In fact, these tribal regions had closer ties with the adjoining regions of Bengal and Burma, than with each other. These areas enjoyed various degrees of independence. All this suddenly changed after India gained independence.

Scholars are of the view that partition and the Chinese takeover of Tibet resulted in the creation of new international political boundaries, replacing the soft territorial frontiers of South Asia. Post-colonial India found itself loaded with a very complex problem in the Northeast. The entire Northeast which once took in an approach to the bordering Tibet, Burma, Bangladesh and Bhutan now had merely a slight link with the residuum of the country with a 21-kilometre wide "Siliguri corridor" in North Bengal, popularly known as "Chicken's Neck." This got the entire region landlocked. The suffocation also influenced the population of the entire northeast of India, causing much discomfort in the area.

During the initial years of independence, three major developments affected India's policy outlook for this newly created frontier region. *First*, the Chinese occupation of Tibet, which contributed to the vanishing of an important buffer zone between India and China and brought the Chinese Army right to the borders of India. *Secondly*, the eruption of the Naga insurgency, which is perhaps India's first ethnic revolt, and thirdly, the change in East Pakistan's political climate, where the communal outlook of the Partition days slowly passed on the way to the Bengali language movement and challenged Pakistani authority. As a consequence of these developments, Muslim colonialism was replaced by Bengali linguistic assertion in East Pakistan, which indirectly influenced India in its nation-building process.

Generally speaking, the Chinese presence on India's borders, and the constant Pakistani support to the Naga, and then to the Mizo, Manipuri and Tripura insurgents, came to be comprehended as a major security threat, and gave rise to an "insecurity syndrome" in New Delhi. Subsequently growing tensions in East Pakistan came to be regarded as an advantage for India. After the Pakistani military operation on the erstwhile East Pakistan had started in March 1971, it became important for India to consider the advantage of the situation to delink China from West Pakistan. India might have thought at that time that cutting Pakistan into two nations would prevent a Sino-Pakistani nexus in the East, and that would help India to protect her Northeast.[27]

It is also important to analyse that the Sino-India war in 1962 left a strong impression on India's policy planners, because the war was not at all favourable to India. The war had presented the significant pre-eminence of China's land army, and its intent to disturb India's Himalayan defences. It raised the threat of a Chinese thrust southwards to the Bay of Bengal, and India realised that as long as West Pakistan had firm control over its eastern wing, i.e., East Pakistan, the fear of a Sino-Pakistani nexus might disturb India's security. It is noteworthy that the 1962 war with China, and the 1965 war with Pakistan, coincided with the outbreak of several ethnic insurgencies in Northeast India. The Mizos, Manipuris and the Tripuris rapidly raised insurgent groups, and set out to trace the course of the Naga insurgency. Gradually, from 1956 onwards, the Nagas had been receiving weapons and training in

East Pakistan. During that year, A. Z. Phizo, one of the major leaders of Naga insurgency, had fled to Dhaka, from where he was flown to London on a false passport provided by the Pakistani authorities.[28] Researchers have pointed out that during 1956-66, Pakistan trained at least eight batches of Naga insurgents (1,700 people in all), and fortified them.[29] Confirmed sources say that during the late 1960s, the Pakistanis also started to supply training and weaponry to the Mizo National Front and the Manipur and Tripura based insurgents. During 1966, insurgent Nagas started going to China for advanced training in guerilla warfare. This was the time when Pakistan-China relations were at the apogee. This is evident from the statement made by the then Indian Foreign Minister on April 8, 1966:

> In the International sphere, the Chinese relationship with several other countries had received setbacks, for example, with Indonesia and Africa .... Chinese are happy with Pakistanis as they explain the Chinese position to the international community.[30]

The growing association of China and Pakistan in promoting these insurgencies annoyed the government in New Delhi. The Indian government felt helpless and immediately resorted to an armed solution to the trouble. But, at the same time, along with the greater deployment of army and paramilitary forces, in an effort to look for a political answer to the problems, New Delhi also tried to initiate dialogues with the subversive groups, particularly the Nagas. In one phase, India was still willing to consider a protectorate status for Nagaland but once the Bengali upsurge started in East Pakistan in early 1971, the Indian state saw a great opportunity in it to solve its northeastern problem. India, initially, was not sure of whether military intervention was the proper course of action in East Pakistan, but it soon convinced the Indian policy planners that the partition of Pakistan was essential for a longstanding solution of India's security concerns in the Northeast.

India noticed clearly that the end of Pakistani domination of its eastern wing, and the emergence of a friendly Bangladesh, would help to stop the Sino-Pakistani nexus, which would eventually stabilise the problems in Northeast India. Thus, Smt. Indira Gandhi, the then Prime Minister of India, took absolute advantage of the situation and helped East Pakistan to fight the war against West Pakistan and played an important role in the formation of Bangladesh, in the year 1971. A non-hostile Bangladesh instead of a hostile East Pakistan was considered more desirable by India during this time. Given the encouragement being offered on and off to centrifugal elements in India's northeastern states from East Pakistani bases, it was natural for New Delhi to support the liberation movement which, in addition, had a powerful humanistic rationale in the context of Pakistan's denial of democratic rights to the Bengali-speaking population. The cultural and emotional sympathy of the people of West Bengal for the East Pakistanis buttressed these considerations.[31]

With the emergence of Bangladesh, the security scenario in Northeast India began to undergo a monumental variety. Within four years of the formation of Bangladesh, Sikkim was merged with India in 1975 in controversial circumstances. In the same year, the *Shillong Accord* was signed with a section of Naga insurgents. As a result, the breakaway group of the Naga National Council soon resumed its armed activities. This breakaway group, known as the National Socialist Council of Nagaland (NSCN), was largely composed of insurgents trained by China. In the midst of this critical situation, in 1976, the Mizo National Front also signed an arrangement with the Indian government in Calcutta. Though it took another ten years to give final shape to the settlement, the part of the Mizo insurgency began to wane in the late 1970s. At the same time this era was noted by the gradual end of the aggressive Chinese patronage to guerrilla groups from Northeast India and Burma (Myanmar). The continuation of Chinese patronage to insurgent groups was ended by the year 1982.

New Delhi was relieved temporarily. The Indian government got the temporary assurance to restore peace in the northeastern region due to the creation of Bangladesh, the limited settlements of the Naga and the Mizo problems and the mounting counter-insurgency operations in the northeastern region of India.

This situation did not go on for a very long time. The situation started to change again when Sheikh Mujibur Rahman, the first prime minister of Bangladesh, was replaced by army generals after his assassination on August 15, 1975. Mujib's death plunged the country into many years of political agitation. The coup leaders were soon overthrown and a series of counter-coups and political assassinations led the country to a poor political fate. After the serial publication of political disturbances, coups and counter-coups, Ziaur Rahman became the seventh President of Bangladesh in 1977. The post-1975 developments in Bangladesh made India anxious about its policy regarding the Northeast area. It is significant to mention here that Indian Prime Minister Indira Gandhi's instant reaction to the Sheikh's assassination was to begin aiding the *Shanti Bahini* guerrillas in the Chittagong Hill Tracts.[32] Almost immediately, Bangladesh's new government headed by Lieutenant General Ziaur Rahman started aiding the insurgents from Northeast India. The guerrilla movements in Northeast India, with the support of Bangladesh, took a new leap forward. With the passage of time these anti-India movements of Northeast India intensified. Their numbers were expected to grow, making Northeast India insecure.

The Change of Indian Policies towards Northeast India

In 1985, Rajiv Gandhi assumed power as Prime Minister of India after the assassination of Smt. Indira Gandhi in the year 1984. Rajiv Gandhi perceived the region of Northeast India meticulously and started to reorient India's policy towards the northeastern region. In the succeeding three years, Rajiv Gandhi's government signed a series of accords with separatist and militant groups in Northeast India. The accords brought an initial end to the violent agitation in Assam, the insurgency in Mizoram and Tripura, and the agitation for a separate state of Gorkhaland in North Bengal. During his regime attempts were made to open negotiations with insurgent groups. In other words, Rajiv Gandhi, as Prime Minister of India, initiated the peace operation in Northeast India decades after the independence of India. The Indian government during this time received positive attention both nationally and internationally. Rajiv Gandhi realised the need for political settlements of the disputes. He changed government policy away from military action and focused primarily on political settlements. Rajiv Gandhi's initial mission towards establishing peace in Northeast India did not last long. During the late 1980s the demand for a separate Bodo State started. All Bodo Students Union under the leadership of Upendranath Brahma, intensified the agitation for a separate Bodo State in some parts of Assam after the 20th Convention of the All-Bodo Students Union held in December 1987. The agitation was set by the regular use of explosives on public transport, road and rail bridges. The Bodo agitation continued to fester until 1993, when an accord was ratified with the Bodos on New Delhi's initiative. The terms of the agreement being the same, it could not hold for long and, as a result, Bodo insurgent groups are still operating in the western and central areas of Assam.

Rajiv Gandhi's fall from power and the coming to power of Prime Minister Viswanath Pratap Singh, and later Prime Minister Chandrashekhar, marked the return of military operations in the northeastern region. The Chandrashekhar government gave the green signal for the first major counter-insurgency operation in Assam, popularly known as *Operation Bajrang*. This operation was launched against the United Liberation Front of Assam (ULFA), which had become an influential force in the late 1980s, and had unleashed a campaign of terror and extortion to mobilise its insurgent forces.

This was also the time when the NSCN started developing several groups elsewhere in the Northeast by consciously supporting them. In Tripura, new insurgent groups like the *All-Tripura Tiger Force* and the *National Liberation front of Tripura* emerged. Insurgency in the Imphal valley now manifested itself through several groups, but the activities of the People's Liberation Army got intensified. Likewise, the threat of an insurgent consolidation also emerged in the security scenario in Northeast India, as the Naga insurgent groups tried to get their own underground alliances. While the *Khaplang* group of the NSCN brought together ULFA and the United National Liberation Front (UNLF) of Manipur into the rather short-lived Indo-Burma Revolutionary Front, the *Isaac Muivah* group of the NSCN roped in the Bodo Security Force (which is now known as the National Democratic Front of Bodoland), the National Liberation Front of Tripura, and some smaller tribal insurgent groups into an informal alliance.

During the 1990s, three other developments in and around the Northeast came to be seen as security threats by Indian defence planners: (a) China during this time started to influence Myanmar both economically and politically; (b) The resurgence of insurgent movements in Northeast India, and it was apparent at the time that there was a support extended to these groups by Pakistan's Inter-Services Intelligence (or ISI) to the northeastern insurgent groups. During this time a new sea route was opened for arms smuggling from Southeast Asia's illegal markets to Northeast India; and (c) The revival of the use of Bangladesh territory by insurgents, with the support of certain anti-Indian elements in that country. The Chinese had come out as the most important suppliers of military instruments to Myanmar's military government. China had also reportedly secured radar, refit and refuel facilities at the Myanmarese ports of Haingyi, the Cocos Islands, and Mergui. The naval unit of the pro-Indian insurgent group, the *National Unity Party of Arakan*, discovered Chinese survey activity around the island of Kyaw Pyu off the Arakan coast, suggesting that the Chinese might be expected to establish another naval base in the Bay of Bengal. The Chinese threat to Indian security, so long considered as a land-based one, added a naval dimension to it. At that time many conceived that China's ambition to produce a blue-water Navy would mean that Calcutta (now Kolkata), Madras and Visakhapatnam (Vizag) would be directly under Chinese missile threats in near future. This is predicted from China's increased missile technology in recent years. In sum, in addition to the Northeast, where the Chinese threat remains, Government of India became worried about the protection of the Andaman and Nicobar Islands, and the country's eastern coastal areas. In the 1990s, as indicated earlier, ULFA, NSCN and other insurgent groups of the Northeast developed contacts with Pakistan's intelligence agency. What was more important was the issue of a new weapons procurement source frequently used by the insurgent groups. The involvement of the northeastern terrorist groups with the illegal markets of Thailand became evident. It likewise was clear that Bangladesh's former military rulers provided the insurgents from Northeast India shelter and material to survive. Most insurgent leaders of Northeast India, who have since been arrested, carried Bangladeshi passports. For example, Anup Chetia (aka Golap Barua, Sunil Barua, Bhaijan and Ahmed) (whose prison term ended in 2003), was arrested in Dhaka on December 21, 1997 on charges of violating the Foreigners Act and the Passports Act of the country. Two of Chetia's associates, identified as Babul Sharma and Laxmi Prasad, were also arrested along with him in the year 1997.[33] The Bangladesh government during the 1990s was fully cognizant of the actions of Manipuri insurgents. As a consequence, the Indian government had stepped up operations against the rebels in the Northeast. Most insurgent organisations, with the exception of ULFA and the Manipuri groups, began to attack ethnic groups whom they perceived as enemies. There was a widespread feeling in India that while Awami League desired friendly relations with India, there were undercurrents of hostility in the approach of the Bangladesh Nationalist

Party (BNP) on relations with India. It was said that the BNP had a link with Pakistan's ISI. They jointly assisted and trained insurgent groups operating in India's Northeastern States, including the ULFA in Assam, the NSCN in Nagaland and the PLA in Manipur. The Indian and Myanmar armed forces had to conduct a coordinated operation in May 1995 to deal with the infiltration of such groups promoted and assisted by the Bangladesh Government. Today, it should be apparent to enlightened sections of the Bangladesh Government that, with the international community now increasingly hostile to terrorism, and the ISI itself being recognised globally as an organisation promoting terrorism, there is little to be gained by Bangladesh in allowing its soil to be used for cross-border terrorism. It is important for Bangladesh to understand that friendly relations with India and support for Indian insurgent groups cannot go hand in hand.[34]

It was the time when the insurgent groups in Tripura regularly attacked villages of Bengali settlers, the Naga insurgents attacked the Kukis and vice versa, and the Bodo insurgents attacked the non-Bodo settlements. Creating compact population zones to support requirements for ethnic homelands has become part and parcel of the armed separatist movements in Northeast India. The Indian policymakers realised that Indian security concerns in the Northeast can be best addressed by mix of military action and political negotiation with the insurgent organisations, along with constant monitoring of Chinese military and diplomatic activities in countries bordering Northeast India, by cutting the sources of supply of weapons and funds to insurgents, and by developing a strong legitimate economy in the region, sustained by large-scale Indian and foreign investment, which would prevent the growth of a smuggling-oriented economy. Thus, till today governmental policies do not encourage international intervention in any form, in any conflict resolution procedures in the northeastern region, though mediated developmental interventions are sanctioned.[35]

Initiation of Look East Policy of India

It is in this backdrop, during the year 1991 when he became Prime Minister of India, that Dr. P. V. Narasimha Rao wanted to bring certain changes in the Policy towards the northeastern region, in the midst of the crisis that the Government of India was facing concerning the northeastern region. Dr. Rao developed India's Look East Policy. India's Look East Policy is not merely an external economic policy that India had initiated. It is also a strategic shift in India's vision of the world and India's place in the evolving global economic organisation. In many ways the post-Cold War external environment of a globalising world gave India the chance to improve dealings with all major powers. It was also the time when India witnessed that there were not too many political rivals who could disturb India's ambition. Thus, in the year 1991, India launched its Look East Policy which became one of the major features of India's Foreign Policy in subsequent years. This also coincided with the period when India had launched the reform-oriented policies in the economic sphere.

With India's antagonism towards Pakistan and with its confused perception towards China, the Southeast Asian region did not figure much in its foreign policy till the early 1990s. After 1990, India realised the potential of Southeast Asia and realised too that the region was going to emerge as a growing market with tremendous potential with countries like Malaysia, Singapore and Indonesia. India had never before concentrated much on China's involvement in the region, and now India realised the reality that China had already extended itself deeply in most of the Southeast Asian countries by virtue of China's developed and aggressive diplomacy. Though some analysts pointed out that by launching this policy India was trying to balance China's influence in this region, India had often repeated the fact, in different ways, that it was not willing to antagonise China in any manner. Indian policymakers understood that it was time to extend beyond the confines of SAARC if it had to get the benefits of the economic potential of Southeast Asia and prove itself to be a regional force. In other words, India's Look East Policy marked a shift of strategic importance and helped India to develop its own perspective of Southeast Asia and Asia-Pacific. "Look East Policy" was an endeavour to forge closer and deeper economic integration with its eastern neighbours as a component of the new *realpolitik.* The engagement with the Association of Southeast Asian Nations (ASEAN) was also a part of the recognition of the economic importance of Southeast Asia to the country's national interests.[36]

In short, India's newest and alternative approach towards the region East of India was regarded as the "Look East Policy." It would be worthy to call up the scenario that existed when the Look East Policy was initiated. First, the decomposition of the Soviet Union marked the end of the Cold War. Secondly, a dramatically changing global scenario began to emerge with new equations and new relationships clearly on the horizon. Thirdly, at this time the United States became the sole global power. Fourthly, a rising China emerged as an increasingly significant player in East Asia. Fifthly, Japan came to a point of economic crisis and was under severe US criticism for its apathy in the first Gulf War and, thus, uncertain and confused about how to handle its relations with ASEAN, China and the United States. The ASEAN countries had dramatically transformed their economies by opening up to each other and got upward with the strategy of engaging China by forging increasingly close economic ties with it, and developed an increasing web of regional institutional linkages. On the other hand, it may be noted that ASEAN had tried to engage India earlier but had not been successful. Meanwhile, India lost its only friend of international strategic consequence, the Soviet Union, and found itself marginalised from the global mainstream in both the economic and political domains. Also, India's relation with the Southeast Asian nations was in poor shape. India's financial and economic condition was also not in good shape at this time. All these factors compelled India to embark on its economic reforms in

1991. India initiated reforms to restructure, deregulate, and liberalise its economic organisation. Whereas China's control in Southeast Asia became an important concern for India. China had provided military support to all of India's neighbours and significant assistance to Pakistan for its nuclear programme. This had been a serious destabilising factor for India. Further, China's rising presence in Southeast Asia had posed serious security concerns in India. In regard to China, India realised that a country in control of the Indo-China region would threaten India's security, and with China's tremendous presence in Southeast Asia, the threat may come from as many Southeast Asian states that have borders adjoining India. As a consequence, India has tried to improve its interaction with Southeast Asia by rebuilding its long-lost links with ASEAN. The Look East Policy represented the Indian response to this new and changing strategic milieu at the grassroots level. India's Look East Policy was a much needed policy because it dovetailed with[37] ASEAN'S fundamental strategic requirements. The fact is that ASEAN had always wanted India to be involved in the field, but it was India that had been reluctant and rejected ASEAN's overtures while continuing to pursue policies which ensured engagement. Thus, when India launched its Look East Policy the ASEAN nations appreciated it and responded favourably to it through the decision to accord sectoral dialogue partner status to India in 1992. Once India had used up the first step, it is the ASEAN that deserves greater credit for engaging India forward to the heights of relationship as it is today. It is particularly noteworthy that ASEAN's decision to accord full dialogue partner status to India in 1995 at the ASEAN summit in Thailand was made without India being given any prior indications whatsoever. Thereafter, in 1996 India was duly accepted as a full and normal member of the ASEAN Regional Forum (ARF). In the year 2002, on November 5, First ASEAN-India Summit took place. In the joint statement issued, it was noted that:

> ASEAN and India committed themselves to jointly contribute to the promotion of peace, stability and development in the Asia-Pacific region and the world, and respond positively to the challenges of a dynamic regional and international environment.[38]

The new geopolitical imagination set off by the new policy thinking envisages a space that seemingly refuses to be bound by the present geography of the Northeast inasmuch as it promises to propagate across the international borders of the countries of Southeast Asia through such Frontline states as Myanmar and Bangladesh. India realised that a comprehensive policy is required for the development of Northeast India and that cannot be done without involving the neighbouring states, Bangladesh and Myanmar. Also, India realised that there is a tremendous growth taking place in the Yunnan district of China which might help positively for the development of the northeastern region of India. And so, India started to perceive the adjacent countries within the purview of its Look East Policy. Thus, the extended Northeast, as being officially imagined, would have a positive effect in so far as it offered a solid ground to the alternative modalities of imagining the Northeast. In simple terms, the Northeast of India is the space between two subregions of Asia—South Asia and Southeast Asia. Both these regions are changing rapidly, marked by tremendous economic growth and development. For various reasons, India till the 1990s had not been able to leverage the various opportunities that this subregion of India had to offer. Gradually, as pointed out earlier, India started to exploit the opportunities for its northeastern region, and started to explore the natural and human resources of the northeastern states. Today's challenge is to harness these opportunities to ensure that growth and development do not bypass this region but pass by this section.

There has been a growing realisation by Indian policymakers that development of physical connectivity with Southeast Asia is a prerequisite to fully harnessing the opportunities provided by Look East Policy. In parliamentary law to create the "Look East Policy" (even the creation of bodies like North East Council [NEC] and Ministry, like Ministry of Development of North Eastern Region [MDONER]) relevant for the region, India has put greater emphasis on increasing connectivity through all the possible modes of infrastructure development, such as land routes, railways, air connectivity, waterways, energy infrastructure development, both in the study of hydroelectric and hydrocarbon, and telecommunication linkages. The important ongoing and potential infrastructure projects in this regard are the roadway between Moreh, Tamu and Kalewa Road, the Trilateral Highway, Trans Asian Highway between the three countries like India, Myanmar and Thailand, India-Myanmar rail linkages, Kaladan Multimodal project, the Stilwell road, Myanmar-India-Bangladesh gas and oil pipeline, Tamanthi Hydroelectricity project and optical fibre network between Northeast India and Southeast Asia.[39] The Northeast should be included in several subregional initiatives, such as the BIMSTEC, Bangladesh-China-India and Myanmar (BCIM), Mekong Ganga Cooperation and Kunming initiative, as a separate economic entity, which, in turn, would facilitate the harnessing of available regional economic opportunities. The bottom line is that the idea of enhancing connectivity between Northeast and Southeast Asia is a welcome step and curbs the potential to change the social and economic landscape of the region. But to initiate this effectively it should be supplemented by efforts to prepare the Northeast for this opportunity.[40] It is a fact that by gradually integrating this region through cross-border market access, the Northeastern states can become the melting point between the Indian economy and Southeast Asia (also the Asia-Pacific Region), which is undoubtedly the fastest developing and most dynamic area in the world.

Conclusion

In this chapter we have discussed the demographic and the ethnological features of Northeast India. Along with this a historical representation of the region has also been made. Thus, it is clear from the discussion that today, what is important is to establish a link between the development and Northeast India which can bring peace and prosperity in the region. It is desirable on the part of the Government to discuss more freely with the local stakeholders of the region. This will help in the process of confidence building and more confidence of the people of northeastern region can be deduced. To start with we have to keep in mind that if the Indian government really wants to establish peace in the Northeastern Region they have to retain the following premises in mind: (a) addressing inter-tribal hostility and competition that is present in the region; (b) more connections must be made by the government, both officially and informally, to convince the insurgent group in the neighbourhood about the advantages of remaining within India's federal system; (c) it is important for policymakers to understand that identities are neither sacrosanct nor static, and as such are no longer cultural artefacts anymore. It is important for policymakers to have the patience to deal with the stakeholders convincing them about the need of maturation in the Northeastern area. It is significant to read repeatedly that India's Look East Policy cannot bypass Northeastern region of India; (d) excess dependence on the elite groups of the area must be brought down. The elites have their own pursuits, which may not serve the interest of the neighbourhood. Recruitment of local people has to be made at the highest stage of government bureaux; (e) a complete survey of displacement, conditions of the local stakeholders like health, instruction and so on has to be made before the implementation of any development projects; and (f) an urgent industrial policy of the Government of India has to originate in the northeastern region which will also include the innovative initiatives like the construction of a sports university in Mizoram or Manipur, use of the rivers of the region for tourism purposes, and the like.

The hegemonic arrogance based on racial, cultural, national, oppression or fascist tendencies cannot be sustained for long. Likewise, democracy, secularism, federalism, and the policy to live and let live with respect to coexistence of subnational or ethnic groups ensures solidarity and integrity of the national and/or federal state. Bringing this into account, Government of India has to administer the region with confidence and faith. At the same time, patience and tolerance are also needed to understand the region along with the theatrical role of the Government. Instead of commanding the region with armed mechanisms more initiatives have to be asked for to tackle the bureaucracy, army and the politicians of the area. Initiatives have to be adopted to reduce or, if possible to eliminate, corruption from the part which is generally managed by the elites who enjoy all the political and administrative forces. This only can assist the area to develop and can develop a nexus between the stakeholders and the regime which will finally facilitate the implementation of the Government of India's Look East Policy more effectively. In Northeast India today, there is an ideological struggle between the indigenous people and the ruling classes like the political leaders, bureaucrats and others. It is now time for the political leadership to be associated with the local people in exhaustive and pluralist form.

Notes

1. B. G. Verghese, "Unfinished Business in the Northeast: Priorities towards Restructuring, Reform, Reconciliation and Resurgence," Seventh Kamal Kumari Lecture, 2001, http://www.freeindiamedia.com/economy/19_june_economy.htm (Accessed July 15, 2014).
2. On July 2, 2008, the Prime Minister released the North Eastern Region Vision 2020, a document which identifies various challenges as well as the strategies required to bring about peace and prosperity in the North Eastern Region by 2020. The core theme of Vision 2020 is that the people of the North East nurture an urgent desire to march on the path of economic, social and cultural progress towards prosperity and well-being, to participate in governance and determine the allocation of public resources and public services they receive.
3. Dr. Shashi Tharoor in his Keynote address delivered at the International Conference on Northeast India in BIMSTEC: From Land Locked to Land Linked, held in Shillong between April 8-10, 2010 organised by the Jadavpur Association of International Relations, supported by the Ministry of External Affairs, Government of India.
4. Ibid.
5. Sharif M. Shuja, "An ethnic Indian quandary: Northeast India—a case study of ethnic provincialism." *Harvard Asia Pacific Review*, 2(2001):55. eLibrary. Web. October 5, 2014.

6. Ibid.
7. Julien Levesque, "Northeast in India's Look East Policy," Institute of Peace and Conflict Studies, no: 2558, May 6, 2008.
8. Sikkim was integrated as the eighth North Eastern Council state in 2002. For details refer North Eastern Council (Amendment Act), 2002.
9. Arunachal Pradesh, meaning "Land of the Rising Sun," has long been a known region of the Indian subcontinent, receiving mention in such ancient Hindu literature as the Kalika-Purana and the epic poems, Mahabharata and Ramayana. Formerly recognised as the North East Frontier Agency (from the British colonial era), the region became the Indian union territory of Arunachal Pradesh in 1972, and in 1987 it became an Indian nation. The area, however, has been the topic of an ongoing sovereignty dispute between India and China.
10. Manipur was one of the princely states of British India. After independence, on September 21, 1949, Maharaja Budhachandra signed a Treaty of Accession merging the kingdom into India.
11. Meghalaya was previously part of Assam, but on January 21, 1972, the districts of Khasi, Garo and Jaintia hills became the young state of Meghalaya.
12. A constitution Amendment Bill conferred statehood on Mizoram. The Bill was passed in the Lok Sabha on August 5, 1986. The formalisation of Mizoram State took place on February 20, 1987. Chief Secretary Lalkhama read out the proclamation of statehood at a public meeting organised at Aizawl's Parade Ground. Prime Minister Rajiv Gandhi inaugurated the new state and Hiteshwar Saikia was appointed as Governor of Mizoram.
13. After the independence of India in 1947, the area remained a portion of the state of Assam. Nagaland attained statehood with the act of the state of Nagaland Act in 1962 passed by the Indian Parliament on December 1, 1963, and Kohima was declared as the state capital. After elections in January 1964, the first democratically elected Nagaland Legislative Assembly was instituted on February 11, 1964.
14. The region of modern Tripura was ruled for several centuries by the Tripuri dynasty. It was a princely state during British rule, and joined the new independent India in 1949.
15. For details on this refer: A. N. M. Irshad Ali and Indranoshee Das, "Tribal Situation in North East India," *Studies of Tribes and Tribals*, 1(2) (2003): 141-48.
16. The "scheduled tribes" only refer to the tribes listed in the Sixth Schedule of the Indian Constitution, and do not reflect the real complexity of the cultural mosaic of the neighbourhood, which covers over 400 distinct tribal and sub-tribal groupings. It is to be pointed out here that the phrase "tribe" is one of the most contested terms, particularly in India.
17. The 2001 Census has made it more specific on the inclusion of scheduled tribes. It is expressed as in Article 342 which provides for specification of tribes or tribal communities or part of or groups within tribes or tribal communities which are deemed to be for the purposes of the Constitution the scheduled tribes in relation to that of the state or union territory.
18. The treaty was signed on February 24, 1826, nearly two years after the war formally broke out on March 5, 1824, by General Sir Archibald Campbell on the British side, and by Governor of Legaing, Maha Min Hla Kyaw Htin from the Burmese side.
19. Raile Rocky, "Tribes and Tribal Studies in North East: Deconstructing the Philosophy of Colonial Methodology," *Journal of Tribal Intellectual Collective India* (ISSN 2321 5437), vol.1 issue 2, no. 2, December 2013, pp. 25-37.

20. http://tribal.nic.in/WriteReadData/CMS/Documents/201306110208002203443DemographicStatusofScheduledTribePopulationofIndia.pdf (Accessed on July 27, 2014).
21. The Lushei, being one of the major tribes of the Mizo people, influenced neighbouring, smaller tribes, such as the Lai/Pawih, the Ralte, the Hmar, the Paite and the Rangte/Gangte.
22. For details on this, see Keihawla Sailo, *Golden History of Lushai Hills* (Aizawl: Synod Press, 2011), pp. 26-27.
23. Ibid., p. 116.
24. Ibid.
25. Sharif M. Shuja, "An ethnic Indian quandary: Northeast India—a case study of ethnic provincialism," *Harvard Asia Pacific Review*, 2(2001):55.
26. For details, see http://cdpsindia.org/ne_insurgency.asp (Accessed on July 16, 2014).
27. Subir Bhaumik, 1996, quoting P. N. Banerji, Joint Secretary (East) in the Research and Analysis Wing (RAW), in *Insurgent Crossfire: Northeast India* (New Delhi: Lancer Books: 1996), p. 52.
28. Nirmal Nibedon, *Night of the Guerrillas* (New Delhi: Lancer Books, 1995), p. 90.
29. B. N. Pakem (ed.), quoting the DGMI Status Report 1967 in "External Linkages of Insurgency in Northeast India," in *Insurgency In Northeast India* (New Delhi: Omsons, 1967), p. 934.
30. Near Verbatim Report of the Foreign Minister's Informal Press Briefing to Indian Press Correspondents on April 8, 1966 at 4.00 p.m. at South Block, in Avtar Singh Bhasin, *India-Pakistan Relations: 1947-2007*, Ministry of External Affairs: Government of India, 2012, p. 1154.
31. J. N. Dixit, *Makers of India's Foreign Policy* (New Delhi: HarperCollins Publishers, 2004), p. 131.
32. A detailed account of the Indian sponsorship to the Shanti Bahini rebel force is available in *Insurgent Cross fire: Northeast India*, pp. 245-306.
33. "Bangladesh to hand over Indian separatist in exchange for murder accused." BBC Monitoring South Asia, August 24, 2014.
34. "India: Prospects for India-Bangladesh relations," *Businessline*, 2001, November 08: 1.
35. Subir Bhaumik, "Insurgency in the North East," *Bharat Rakshak Monitor*, vol. 5(2), September-October, 2002.
36. Thongkholal Haokip, "India's Look East Policy," *Third Concept—An International Journal of Ideas*, vol. 25, no. 291, May 2011: p. 7.
37. Ranjit Gupta, "India's 'Look East' Policy" in *Indian Foreign Policy: Challenges and Opportunities*, Foreign Service Institute: New Delhi, 2007: pp. 351-81.
38. Joint Statement issued on the First ASEAN-INDIA Summit held at Phnom Penh, Cambodia, November 5, 2002.
39. "STATES: Meet highlights potential of North-East," *Businessline*, April 12, 2010.
40. Julien Levesque, "Northeast in India's Look East Policy," *Institute of Peace and Conflict Studies*, no. 2558, May 2008, p. 6.

2

FROM "LOOK EAST" TO "ACT EAST": A CRITICAL ANALYSIS OF INDIA'S LOOK EAST POLICY

Introduction

The present government, which came to power in May 2014, has accorded high priority to India's Look East Policy (LEP). India's interest in the countries to its east is evident from the fact that it has undergone a paradigm shift in policy and is moving away from "Look East" approach to "Act East" mode. India is not merely "Looking East" but is now "Acting East," thus revising the title to "India's Act-East Policy." The Look East Policy is now known as the Act East Policy.[1] However, by changing the name of India's Asia policy from Look East to Act East, Prime Minister Narendra Modi was signalling that he would be more proactive and purposeful than his predecessors in the region. To be sure, New Delhi has made much progress in reconnecting with Asia since the early 1990s. Yet the gap between potential and reality has steadily grown. So has the gulf between rising regional expectations of an Indian role in Asia and the political will in Delhi to measure up.[2] Regardless of India's instincts and intentions, Delhi has much to do before its Act East policy gains credibility in Asia—from the creation of a more business-friendly environment to faster implementation of trans-border projects; from visa liberalisation to expanding defence cooperation. The East has its arms open and is ready to embrace India, but sometimes it has been seen that the will of India remained tied by Delhi's political and bureaucratic inertia.[3]

Any nation that undertakes a change of course in its foreign policy does so under a certain set of circumstances, both internal and external. This usually happens when the international power stability is distressed by external catastrophic events, such as the collapse of the Soviet Union or the less tragic and more steady disequilibrium created by the rise of China. When the world enters such phases of disequilibrium in the international power structure, it forces nations into making policy manoeuvres, to protect its perceived national interest. Internal developments also impact upon foreign policy. In fact any nation's foreign policy is primarily driven by domestic priorities.[4] It is true today that the International power set-up is undergoing a phase of power disequilibrium. Traditional ideas like empires, revolutions, imperialism, colonialism and wars that marked the passage of the last three centuries are no more effective today. The earlier phases were marked by new structures, which were highly integrated technologically, intimately connected with digital information flowing at the speed of light in all directions. This newly emerged power structure has given rise to the multipolar world with a few dominant powers, diminishing the idea of superpower. These few dominant powers are developing small groups based on their demographic and economic depth. In fact, one such grouping is the G-20, comprising the top 20 countries in the world as per their GDP, which is now a regular forum for discussing economic and fiscal policies.[5]

In other words, no one country wants to be a superpower today. The USA is a receding power, approaching to *lead from behind*[6] and delegating more security and military responsibilities to its allies. Similarly, Europe is in the throes of an economic downturn and busy trying to save the Euro and the imploding economies of Greece and other southern European states. The other great powers are not in a position to take over the role of a global hegemon, or a manager, and run the world as per a particular template or ideology. In reaction to China's rise, China is rather deliberate in not giving way beyond a degree because it worries about other major powers joining together to restrain it, if not check it.

Another significant mark of the post-Cold War world is the acceptance of liberal market policies by virtually all states including China, Russia, Vietnam, India, Brazil, Egypt, Japan, Germany, France, Nigeria, South Africa and many more.

Initiation of India's Look East Policy

In defining the context, let us recall that more than two decades ago, at a lecture in Singapore in September 1994, Prime Minister Narasimha Rao adumbrated a vision of establishing closer relations with the countries of the Association of Southeast Asian Nations or ASEAN. This vision came to be called the *Look East Policy* or LEP.[7] The renewed vision to look for closer relations with states in India's extended eastern neighbourhood was quintessentially India's response to domestic economic challenges and an external environment, punctuated by a unipolar world, brought about by the prostration of the Soviet Union and the death of the Cold War. Hence the economic reforms of 1991 and the opening up of India's economy provided the impetus for reworking India's foreign policy. Confronted with multiple problems, economic and political, India adopted two parallel new paths—a domestic policy path of economic liberalisation and the external policy path of the LEP to help expand India's trade and investment in the dynamic ASEAN region. These two choices have transformed India's economy and foreign policy in the past 20 years. Prime Minister Rao's statement in 1994 in Singapore is justifiably seen as a major shift in Indian diplomacy, comparable to non-alignment during the Cold War epoch. The economic reforms, initiated in 1991, started the cognitive operation of consolidation of the Indian economy with the planetary economic system. India's search for expanding global markets for Indian products, services and investments led to the LEP. It was a legitimate consequence of domestic compulsions and a changed external environment.

As early as 1992, India had joined a limited "Sectoral Dialogue" with the 10-country grouping ASEAN. India's strategic engagement with ASEAN began with India's membership of the ASEAN Regional Forum (ARF) in 1996. ASEAN overruled objections from some of its other partners, particularly China, on India's admission to the ARF. The LEP, thereafter, started merging trade and economic involvement with issues of geostrategic significance. The geographical outreach extended further eastwards towards Australia and Oceania. A variety of institutions became operational for holding regular dialogue. Amongst this, the annual summit became the highest body. Separately, India is also a member of ASEAN Defence Ministers Meeting (ADMM) + 8 where the focus is on security, defence and strategic issues. As a Strategic Partner of ASEAN, India is actively associated with various ASEAN-led fora dealing with defence and strategic issues. These include the East Asia Summit, the ASEAN Regional Forum, ADDM+ (ASEAN Defence Ministers Meeting Plus) and the Expanded ASEAN Maritime Forum. India's defence ties with the region have expanded significantly. India also has bilateral defence cooperation activities with ASEAN and other regional countries.

Still, India's Look East Policy received a new dimension during the Vajpayee era, when Atal Behari Vajpayee became the Prime Minister of India in 1998 after NDA won the elections. It is particularly from this time that India took off following the policy of Constructive Engagement with Myanmar, since Myanmar became a member of ASEAN in the year 1997, and therefore, through Myanmar, India wants to establish economic linkages with other ASEAN members like Thailand, Singapore, Malaysia, Indonesia and others. In fact, Myanmar shares a 1,643 kilometre-long boundary line with India along the states of Manipur, Mizoram, Nagaland and Arunachal Pradesh, and hence it will not be a misunderstanding to say that Myanmar acts as a gateway to the Southeast Asian region of the Indian Republic. If we proceed back to history, we will find that India's relations with Myanmar have gone through loads of ups and piles. Especially the military junta, that had ruled Myanmar for several years, was not on serious terms with India, since the latter had always defended the pro-democratic movements in Myanmar. However, after the 1990s the situation changed, leading to the improvement in India-Myanmar relations to a certain extent, though interstate tensions remain. Moreover, the signing of the BIMSTEC in 1997 during the premiership of I. K. Gujral, and later, that of the Mekong-Ganga cooperation in 2000 during the Vajpayee period, are clear evidence of India's ASEAN engagement, or rather India's constructive engagement in Myanmar. The most important and fruitful ramification of this engagement was visible when India was made the Summit Level Partner of ASEAN in 2002. It was, perhaps, for this reason that Yashwant Sinha, the then Foreign Minister of India, marked the year 2002 as the beginning of the "Second Phase" of India's Look East Policy.

Meanwhile, the year 2004 marked the Dr. Manmohan Singh era in Indian politics. Dr. Singh was keen to build up relations with the Southeast Asian nations during his tenure, especially with Myanmar and Vietnam. Besides BIMSTEC and Mekong-Ganga Cooperation, India has initiated many important projects with Myanmar, such as the opening of Tamu-Kalewa-Kalemyo Highway (popularly known as Indo-Myanmar Friendship Road), the Tamantha river-valley project, gas line projects in the Arakan region. India is only too well aware about the Sittwe Route of Myanmar, since control over this route will make India an easy entry to the region of Southeast Asia as a whole. In fact, after the democratisation of Myanmar in 2013, the Indian government has offered a loan of US $500 million to Myanmar for the political reconstruction of the nation. Likewise, the Manmohan government has also maintained cordial relations with Vietnam, which is apparent from the various defence agreements which have been contracted between the Indian and the Vietnamese governments. Besides, India-Vietnam joint venture in oil exploration in South China Sea is a significant step taken towards the economic growth of the nation. Nevertheless, the year 2009 can be seen as a milestone, since in this year India and ASEAN finally signed Free Trade Agreement (FTA) in goods, besides revising the Maritime Doctrine of 2004. As an outcome of this doctrine, Indian ships can now sail from the South China Sea to the Indian Ocean, which was not easily possible in the late age.[8]

From Look East to Act East

Today, after the coming of the BJP-led NDA regime in power in May 2014, many new concepts and ideas have been inaugurated in the foreign policy of India, one of which is the "Act East" policy. The present regime, under the Prime Ministership of Narendra Modi, aims at getting connected with Indians residing overseas and requires to rejuvenate India's relations with the ASEAN members, which is further apparent from the lectures given by Modi during his various press conferences or foreign tours. In fact Sushma Swaraj, the External Affairs Minister of India, during her official tour in Hanoi on August 2014, has clarified the "Act East" policy of Modi by stating that the policy of "Act East" would replace the age-old Look East Policy, since it is not enough to Look East but to Act East, i.e., to put India's Look East policy into action. This is, indeed, looked upon by many scholars as an active step taken forward with regard to India's Look East Policy in recent times. In fact, the Act East Policy has also been highlighted by Narendra Modi at the 12th ASEAN-India Summit held in Nay Pyi Taw of Myanmar in November 2014, where the Indian Prime Minister has also emphasised the three "C"s—commerce, culture and connectivity. Also, India's presence in the meetings of the ASEAN Regional Forum (ARF) or that of the East Asia Summit (EAS) of 2014—all these events repeatedly herald Modi's Act East Policy, thus revealing India's priority concern for the ASEAN group. In the swiftly changing security dynamics in the region, Indian Prime Minister Narendra Modi rechristened the approach the "Act East" policy, putting forward the importance of also seeking deeper ties with partners such as Japan, Vietnam, South Korea and Australia.[9] Trade and investment are two important pillars of the Act East Policy. ASEAN is India's fourth largest trading partner. Bilateral trade has topped US$ 75 billion in 2013-14, with both sides committing themselves to reach a trade turnover of US$ 100 billion by 2015 and US$ 200 billion by 2022. Beyond ASEAN, the East Asia Summit (EAS) has emerged as the larger institution, with ASEAN as its driver and hub. It includes not only ASEAN member-states but also China, Japan, and South Korea as well as India, Australia and New Zealand. This institution now includes the USA and Russia. Thus, as a part of the Act East policy, India has to nurture bilateral relations with ASEAN countries and others, deepen cooperation with institutions such as BIMSTEC, ASEAN and EAS and to craft strategic understanding with major powers such as China, Russia and the USA on the future of Asia. The architecture of Southeast and East Asian relationships has become complex and so has the evolving architecture of relations between India and countries in these regions. Whether EAS will some day pave the way for the formation of East Asian Community (EAC) or Asian Economic Community (AEC), or eventually to Asian Community (AC), remains to be seen. Besides, India is also a member of Asia-Europe Meeting (ASEM) and is also interested in joining Asia-Pacific Economic Cooperation (APEC).[10] In other words, the LEP's changing profile and its increased geostrategic significance has led to the demand for a more proactive approach which is now referred to as the "Act East" policy. In its essence it means that India has to energise its LEP and act with more dynamism. The appointment of an Indian Ambassador to deal exclusively with ASEAN and the East Asia Summit signals this proactive policy. This aspect has received much attention from Prime Minister Modi's government. The recalibration of the LEP into Act East is visible. At the 12th ASEAN-India Summit, Prime Minister Narendra Modi stated: "Externally, India's 'Look East Policy' has become 'Act East Policy.'"[11] Prime Minister Modi also said that "India's Act East starts with Bangladesh,"[12] firmly indicating that Bangladesh will be integrated with the Act East policy. This is because

Modi's commitment to stability in the South Asian neighbourhood will not necessarily come at the expense of East Asian engagement. India's Northeastern states cannot be easily accessed from the mainland without Bangladesh's cooperation, so positive relations with India's South Asian neighbours will be crucial to enhancing its land connectivity with Southeast Asia.10[13] In addition, since becoming Prime Minister, Modi has advocated a "Look East, Link West Policy" pointing to a broader Indo-Pacific conceptualisation of India's region.[14]

Thus, the LEP's new orientation as the Act East policy is underway. It is in fact a maturing of the LEP. But for the rhetoric to meet reality adequate resources have to be pumped into energising this policy. There are two dimensions to this policy; one, the overland connectivity, and the other, the maritime domain. India has to provide adequate resources to make our country a maritime power in the Indo-Pacific region and pursue the overland option with greater vigour. Myanmar is the key to the future of this policy. Myanmar is India's landbridge to Southeast Asia. The investment climate in Myanmar has improved with a more democratic regime in that country. Trade at the border town of Moreh is opening up and informal trade may soon come down, improving revenue and living conditions in our northeastern states. Myanmar is already India's chief source of imported pulses. India-Myanmar trade has more than doubled in the last seven years and has crossed $2 billion in 2013-14. But India remains Myanmar's distant eleventh trading partner, despite being a neighbour with a 1,700 km shared boundary.[15]

Act East and India's Northeast

The Act East policy has huge significance for India's northeastern states. It is therefore important to emphasise the importance of overland connectivity, since maritime trade bypasses the northeastern region. In the context of cross-border transformation in the northeastern region of India, physical connectivity is a very important component. The security dimension in the northeast of India has had a dampening effect on infrastructure projects and they are facing delays due to political, security and financial problems. Because of security concerns, the only infrastructure projects in the Northeast so far, have been undertaken by the government's own agencies. While the Moreh-Tamu-Kalemayo Road has been completed, other projects like the India-Myanmar-Thailand trilateral highway, Kaladan multi-modal project, Tamanthi hydroelectric project, etc., are facing delays due to political, security and financial problems. Partnerships with the Asian countries such as Japan, Kores, Thailand, Indonesia, Malaysia and Singapore can generate healthy competitive impulses to get some of these projects moving faster is a new focus of the Act East policy. India's Northeast region deserves special mention in her Look East policy. The natural beauty and resources here are ideal for the development of Tourism Industry in states like Manipur, Mizoram, Nagaland, Sikkim, Arunachal Pradesh, etc.

However, the Indian government has been blamed for not giving much attention to this region, and as a result continuous and unaddressed grievances here have finally given rise to a few local insurgent groups, which are inculcating anti-Indian feelings among the local people. Many of these insurgent groups even have their bases in Myanmar, and China has been accused here of supplying arms and weapons to the insurgents, both in India and Myanmar, in order to carry out anti-government movements there. This can be seen as a kind of provocation to regionalism in both the countries, thus endangering their national solidarities. Moreover, Sino-Indian tension surrounding the Indian Ocean is a well-known fact today, and China is now trying to strengthen its hold over Myanmar in order to capture the huge Asian market as well as to expand its foothold in the Indian Ocean through Myanmar.

Another notable problem is the South China Sea issue, which is truly an area of confrontation for India, China, Vietnam, the Philippines and other countries, mainly because of the huge storage of oil, gas and other natural resources in the region. In 2011 India and Vietnam had signed an agreement between them on oil and gas exploration in the South China Sea, which had been opposed by the Chinese Government. In fact, confrontation between Chinese warships and India's INS Airavat in the waters of South China Sea in the same year evoked serious concern in the international scenario. It must be mentioned in this regard that China, after many refusals, had finally signed the "Code of Conduct" with regard to the South China Sea in 2002, and had also become a member of the East Asia Summit by signing the TAC. However, the South China Sea problem, which had subsided since 2002, revived again in 2010 after Hillary Clinton, the then US Secretary of State, declared the South China Sea problem to be an international issue. Tension was somehow averted in the ASEAN Summit meeting in 2012, but the Sino-Indian tension regarding South China Sea still remains unresolved.

Besides, Sino-Indian relations have been embittered by serious border problems since the Cold War period, which includes the Tibet issue, the Kashmir and Arunachal problems, and so on. The Sikkim problem was resolved in 2006, but other problems remain. Keeping in mind the need of the era of globalisation, India has extended its helping hand towards China, which is evident from the events of Sino-Indian cooperation in the forums of BRICS, ASEAN, and so on.

So far as India-Japan relations is concerned, it has been mentioned earlier that India has been sharing a friendly relationship with Japan since the era of pre-independence, and Japan had also helped in India's struggle for freedom. In fact, Japan has remained one of the important trading partners of India for years. Besides, Narendra Modi recently paid a visit to Japan in 2014, which led to the restrengthening of this relationship through the conclusion of several agreements, which affirms the development of "Special Strategic Global Partnership" between the two. In fact, India and Japan have common security concerns in the Indian Ocean as well as in the Asia-Pacific region, for which both have signed a security pact in 2008 during the premiership of Dr. Manmohan Singh. In recent times, the Modi government has carried out negotiations with Japan for the purchase of the "US 2" amphibious aircraft for military purposes, which might have positive ramifications on India-Japan security relations.

Coming to the Northeast, it may be argued that although India's Look East policy is strongly rooted in national interests, it has been aiming towards the strategic importance of India's Northeast region. Prime Minister Narendra Modi, on a recent visit to Tripura, said the northeastern region of India would be made a gateway of Southeast Asia. "An economic corridor would be established using Northeast India, Myanmar and the adjoining regions. Northeast India would be a gateway of Southeast Asia in future," Modi said. He further claimed that the Northeast "would not remain backward now ... As the gateway to Asia, it had the potential to move forward in this century, which was being called the century of Asia ... Towards this end, the government is keen on building modern infrastructure in the Northeast, to unlock its potential." Elucidating the importance of the Northeastern Region, and on why it is important to the Look East-Act East Policy, Dr. Gupte and Yeravdekar noted, "The Northeast region has the potential to play the arrowhead role in evolution of the 'Look East-Act East Policy,' and in fact it would not be wrong to say that looking and acting east will begin from here. South Asian states such as Bangladesh, Nepal and Bhutan are so closely linked with Act East policy that they also need to be considered as part of the policy."

The biggest constraint in the NER, however, has been the poor state of infrastructure, governance and corruption. A number of studies on the Northeast have highlighted the problem of infrastructure, governance and corruption in the region. The vision of trade and prosperity cannot be realised without providing the region with world-class infrastructure and building a system of good governance. Tripura Chief Minister Manik Sarkar has rightly argued, "The NE has not been suffering from lack of natural resources, but the attitude of the Centre has virtually undermined the sentiments of the people ... owing to the absence of proper infrastructure, the full potential of the NE region could not be tapped."[16]

Indeed, infrastructure development is the fundamental prerequisite for the meaningful involvement of the North Eastern Region in India's Act East Policy and Globalisation process. All these will require huge investment; it is therefore imperative that adequate fund flow for public investment needs to be assured. It is urging the policymakers and planners to formulate a comprehensive strategy for the speedy development of the region and deepen the engagement with the ASEAN countries.

Infrastructure projects should be taken up on a war footing without disturbing the social and cultural identities of the various ethnic groups of the region. The present author suggests a special fiscal package for massive public expenditure on infrastructure development and to make available more funds to state governments of the region through federal transfers. The new paradigm must entail a massive expansion of productive capacities of the region's economy. This has acquired urgency, when trade and commerce with neighbours and East and Southeast Asian countries have enhanced and good prospects are waiting for the northeastern region.[17]

At this point in time, the Act East policy appears to be driven by Delhi, and has perhaps not been able to inspire local people to the extent it should. There is enormous potential in Assam and Meghalaya for development. This is why there needs to be inspired imagination. We can imagine Moreh in Manipur becoming a border town with smart hubs for business buttressed by the concept of eco-tourism. This will generate local employment and attract visitors. Arunachal Pradesh and Nagaland are immensely beautiful and people there have great potential, but they often bemoan the lack of opportunity and infrastructure. It is here that long-term vision and imagination are critical; a state that can develop sound infrastructure and business will benefit its people. Community tourism can assist people who are in dire need of resources. This imagination has to be generated and supported by the States which are best equipped to understand local realities. To establish conditions for development and peace, we will have to start locally, today.[18]

India's Northeast region deserves special mention in her Look East policy. The natural beauty and resources here are ideal for the development of Tourism Industry in States like Manipur, Mizoram, Nagaland, Sikkim, Arunachal Pradesh, etc. However, the Indian government has been blamed for not giving much attention to this region, and as a result, continuous and unaddressed grievances here have finally given rise to local insurgent groups, which are inculcating anti-Indian feelings among the local people. Many of these insurgent groups have their bases in Myanmar, and China has been accused of supplying arms and weapons to the insurgents, both in India and Myanmar, in order to carry out anti-government movements there. This can be seen as a kind of provocation to regionalism in both the countries, thus endangering their national solidarities. Moreover, Sino-Indian tension surrounding the Indian Ocean is a well-known fact today, and China is now trying to strengthen its hold on Myanmar in order to capture the huge Asian market as well as to expand its foothold in the Indian Ocean through Myanmar.

On the other hand, connectivity remains a vital issue in the question of India's Act East-Look East Policy. India can connect to NER through Bangladesh, which is one of the most important routes connecting NER with the rest of India. The government of India has certain initiatives. India understands that Bangladesh is one country in South Asia where ending bitterness and hostility towards India is important. At the same time, it is important for India to equip the political faction in Bangladesh moving towards securing peace and democracy. The recent visit of the Indian Prime Minister to Bangladesh on June 6, 2015 started on a positive note. The exchange of enclaves has been done, and the possibility of an agreement on Teesta waters does not seem as remote as it was some years ago. It is important to note here that the land boundary and Teesta issues are residues of history and India is now prudent enough to solve the issues gradually. It is also important to note here that India needs to spend money on Bangladesh's economic development. Unless that is done, the issues that bedevil bilateral relations—illegal migration and conflict over resources—will escalate in the future. If only from the perspective of ensuring its security, India should spend freely on Bangladesh.[19] This is also important for India's connectivity programme within the framework of Act East Policy. As a part of the present connectivity programme of Government of India, Indian Prime Minister and his Bangladeshi counterpart, Sheikh Hasina, on June 6, 2015 flagged off the Kolkata-Dhaka-Agartala bus service marking a historic moment in bilateral relations between the two countries. The Kolkata-Dhaka bus service was introduced in 1999. Since then, there has been a demand for connectivity with Tripura. The successful run of Kolkata-Dhaka service brightened the scope for another service in the northeastern sector. The existing route between Kolkata and Agartala by road has been a complex one with an estimated distance of 1,650 kilometres. The journey through the narrow "chicken neck" territory via Guwahati and Shillong takes around two days. But the new route via Dhaka, Rupganj, Narsingdi, Brahmanberia and Akhaura would bring down the distance to 470 kilometres.[20] This is undoubtedly a positive step towards linking NER with the rest of India contributing to the practical framework of India's Act East Policy.

The Future of Act East Policy

The future of India's Act East policy has to be woven by the twin strands of economic participation and strong security ties. India must build a web of relationships with all nations, including China. With the historic visit of the Emperor and Empress of Japan to India, the Act East policy has gone into a fast lane with respect to Japan, the third biggest economy and a technological power which are already taking on a transformational role in establishing infrastructure in India (Delhi Metro and the Delhi-Mumbai Industrial corridor). Today, security relations are also growing and India and Japan are on the threshold of achieving a civil nuclear accord. Prime Minister Abe of Japan was the Chief Guest for the Republic Day festivities in January 2014. Japan has a key part in our Act East policy as a partner in economic and security cooperation, including defence supplies. The Republic of Korea (ROK) has likewise taken a crucial profile in our insurance. ROK has steadily invested in sectors like automobiles, white goods, electronics and mining, making a mark in the manufacturing sector. Aside from the free trade agreement with ASEAN, India has Comprehensive Economic Partnership Agreements (CEPA) with Japan and Korea. India is a founder member of the East Asia Summit (EAS) and is a member of the ongoing Regional Comprehensive Economic Partnership negotiations which groups together the 10 ASEAN countries, China, Korea, Japan, India, Australia, New Zealand. From the geostrategic point of view, Indonesia and Vietnam are also key countries. India will have to nurture these three crucial relationships because of the added dimension of security, while building a web of relationships with major countries, including China, which is increasingly taking the lead in initiating moves for a larger economic and security architecture in Asia. Act East policy will also have to meet the challenge of how to deal with the proposed Trans-Pacific Partnership (TPP), led by the USA with 12 Asian-Pacific countries that include some ASEAN countries, Japan, Australia and New Zealand. If China joins the TPP, then India will be marginalised since China's trade with ASEAN and the USA is US$ 450 billion and US$ 516 billion respectively. The China-Japan trade volume is over US$ 300 billion. India is way behind but can hope to catch up if India's domestic economic growth picks up and we can sustain a GDP growth rate of 7+%. The other domain from which new challenges to our Act East policy is likely to spring up is security.[21] The rise of China has led to a military build-up in Asia and arms transfers have gone up manifold, underlining the unstable security situation. China's Maritime Silk Route proposal involves building ports and other infrastructure assets in the subcontinent. China is preparing to deploy its maritime capability in the Indian Ocean. India's Act East policy must, therefore, incorporate countervailing measures which build military cooperation with the USA, Japan, Korea, Australia and ASEAN countries. The goal will be to inhibit China's projection of power and at the same time build cooperation on common areas of interest like combating piracy, maritime disaster management and keeping the Sea Lanes of Communication open for trade. India must also leverage its considerable cultural influence to engage all Asian countries. This aspect has so far not been fully leveraged.

The Act East policy has acquired great relevance in the global geostrategic space. Indubitably, it is a pillar of India's foreign policy, competing with our South Asia policy and our policy towards the USA, Russia, China, Japan, the European Union and other emerging economies, giving India the necessary space to play its legitimate role as an emerging great power.

Conclusion

In conclusion, one must have in mind the gradual development of India's Look East Policy, which, though it ran into rough weather during the Cold War period, eventually earned its position in India's foreign policy domain, and today has become one of the priority concerns for Indian policy-shapers. Nevertheless, the involvement of China in the area of Southeast Asia has made the situation sort of complicated. For example, China's support for the local insurgent groups, both in India and in Southeast Asia, or China's growing trade relations with the ASEAN members—these are the upcoming challenges which India has to face while sharing with the ASEAN factor. Consequently, the Indian government has to be extra careful while formulating and implementing its policies in this area. The changes which have been brought about in India's Look East Policy over decades have no doubt aided in the socio-economic development of India, and this has been possible through India's involvement in ASEAN, BIMSTEC and other regional assemblies. Still, how far the Indian government will be successful in realising its Act East Policy by addressing the domestic as well as the international challenges is a matter yet to be called. It is true today that the reality of India-Myanmar land connectivity is increasingly a possibility as militancy and insurgency are on the descent in the Northeast. However, it is also too true that without the development of the Northeastern Region, the Act East Policy cannot be successful. In conditions of strong connectivity, Trilateral Highway still remains an open inquiry and the region is in desperate need of ample development investments. This in turn raises several questions over the progress of Look East Policy and connecting Northeast India to the world, most of which remain unanswered. At the local level also, India has to be more careful in dealing with the insurgents struggling against India to implement its Act East Policy. On June 4, 2015 in a major ambush in Manipur's Chandel district, 11 armymen of 6 Dogra Regiment were killed and 10 others injured in an attack by militants. The attack took place near Moltuk on the Indo-Myanmar border. The ambush was laid by an unidentified terrorist outfit under Tengnoupal Police Station in the territorial dominion. Sources said that the terrorists used heavy firepower in the attempt. The Army convoy was a road opening party and was attacked with rocket propelled grenades (RPGs) and heavy gunfire. If this kind of scenario continues, it will be hard to implement India's Act East Policy. Special attention on the theatrical role of the Government of India is required to remove suspicion and to build confidence in the region where Bangladesh and Myanmar have to play a significant role. It may me mentioned here again that India's "Look East Policy" has long shaped the nation's ties with the Asia-Pacific and the Southeast Asian nations. But Prime Minister Modi now pursues a more ambitious agenda based on stronger ties with Japan, Vietnam, Australia and ASEAN. In many respects, the Prime Minister's approach to the Asia-Pacific builds upon the policies of previous governments. However, his government has intensified its outreach to India's key partners, such as Japan,

Vietnam, Australia and ASEAN. His key goals are to deepen economic ties with the Asia-Pacific in order to boost India's own economic growth, to balance externally against Chinese influence in the Indian Ocean, and to expand India's global role. While the Modi government must work quickly to ensure that "Act East" goes beyond a rebranding of an existing policy, the upgraded policy signals India's intention to assume a greater role in the region. India is certainly wary of China's growing presence in the Indian Ocean and its relationships with India's South Asian neighbours. In light of this, India's Look East Policy can be conceived as part of an external balancing strategy against China. At the same time, Beijing is also displaying wariness towards India's growing relationships with key partners in East and Southeast Asia, particularly with Vietnam and Japan. While it is not in India's interests to engage in direct rivalry with China, it can be expected that an element of competition will continue to characterise the China-India bilateral relationship.

These stresses will also help to reinforce the relevance of investing in India's relationships with collaborators such as ASEAN and Japan. ASEAN will remain a vital part of India's Look East Policy. Chinese assertiveness on territorial disputes has given India the opportunity to enhance its strategic presence in Southeast Asia, and ASEAN states are more and more looking to India to play a balancing role in the area. Bilateral partnerships within individual ASEAN states, such as Vietnam and Indonesia, hold particular promise.

India's relations with Japan are likely to undergo the most change under the Modi government, especially in light of his personal association with Japanese Prime Minister Shinzo Abe. Japan's tense relationship with China has inspired it to reach out to India as a potential strategic partner. Equally the most advanced Asian naval power, and as a possible source of considerable investment and technological assistance, Japan offers India significant partnership opportunities as it switches its focus eastwards.

Indian Prime Minister Narendra Modi's recent visit to China[22] was high on specifics and low on rhetoric. With a stack of 21 business agreements worth more than $22 billion signed, Modi seems to have adopted the advice of foreign policy experts to base Sino-India bilateral relations on a more pragmatic standing. Rather than resorting simply to *Hindi-Chini Bhai Bhai* sentiments, Modi has made it clear that China should be treated more as a "partner" in India's long road to development especially in infrastructure. This visit saw significant government-to-government pacts in railways, mining and minerals, establishing sister-city relations, etc. India even announced an electronic visa on arrival for Chinese visitors. However, during the visit no significant step was taken regarding the boundary issues between the two countries. Although there were talks of setting up a hotline between the military headquarters of the two countries, the Chinese side remained largely silent on India's suggestion that China must reconsider its approach on some of the issues that hold India back from understanding the full potential of India-China partnership. At the same time, there was no response to the Indian PM's proposal for clarifying the *Line of Actual Control* (LAC) or on the *stapled visa policy*[23] to people from Arunachal Pradesh (which China refers to as South Tibet). These are important issues and India needs to find a way to get the Chinese to engage in a resolution of these vital security issues. Presently, India does not have the economic or military power to counter China. However, what India has is its geopolitical importance in Asia, which both the US and China are trying to leverage. India should use this to straighten its relationship with China.

Beijing in recent years is reasserting its military power and activities in the South and East China Sea, while the US is helping its allies and partners to realign themselves militarily. There is a fast-growing defence network in the region comprising China's adversaries whose strategy seems to be to isolate Beijing. Japan, which reinterpreted its Pacifist constitution last year, is now all set to affirm its right to "collective self-denial." This means that Japan could provide military assistance to its allies like the US in a warlike situation. A significant step forward is the rewrite of the Guidelines for US-Japan Defence Cooperation. The revision incorporates cooperation, including defence against ballistic missiles and maritime protection. For Japan it underscores Washington's reassurances that it will stand by Tokyo in case of a military showdown with China. China has gone a step further by enhancing its strategic cooperation with Australia. Japan will now operationally aid Australia, especially in case of any attack on Australian vessels while operating in US military exercises in South China Sea.

According to reports, the US might expand its current training exercises in Southeast Asia, which will include multilateral military exercises in the region. For example, bilateral naval exercises conducted by the US Navy, such as the annual *Cooperation Afloat Readiness and Training* (CARAT), will now call for multiple countries in Southeast and South Asia, including Bangladesh, Brunei, Cambodia, Indonesia, Malaysia, the Philippines, Singapore, Thailand and Timor-Leste. This coincides with India's reinvigorated focus on its "Act East" policy. It is drawing India closer to not only Japan and Australia in the Pacific but also to smaller Southeast Asian nations, most of whom have contended territorial claims with China (like Vietnam). In response to the US-led *Trans-Pacific Partnership* it has likewise come up with competing free trade accords like the *Regional Comprehensive Economic Partnership* (RCEP) that includes ASEAN members apart from Australia, China, India, Japan, New Zealand and South Korea. China's immediate project—the *Silk Road*, the Economic Belt—serves the same motive of bringing countries into the Chinese economic fold. China will find a convergence in India's need for investment to accentuate its growth with its own stake to hold bigger influence on India by offering economic assistance. Beijing has already stated its desire to get India on board in its infrastructural activities as a first step. Beijing will further look at India playing a larger part in its *Asian Infrastructure Investment Bank* (AIIB). China even proposed that areas of common interest could be found in India's "Act East" policy and the *belt and road*[24] initiative. China said that the two countries, India and China, could deepen involvement on the *belt and road*, within the framework of AIIB. Chinese opinion even suggests collaborating in infrastructure and joint ventures by the two nations in Africa, Latin America and West Asia.

Quite evidently Beijing's insistence on common points of overlap between the two countries is to spare China of any friction with India in its *Act East policy*. This is possibly a point India should leverage. China is working with Pakistan to construct a *Sino-Pakistan Economic Corridor* across the Karakoram ranges in Pakistan-occupied Kashmir (PoK) and tying with the Arabian Sea at Gwadar. New Delhi—while being mindful of not appearing as well close to America's rebalance strategy—should use its partnership forged as a result of Act East policy to get Beijing to commit that none of its relationships in India's neighbourhood will cause an untoward impression on the nation. This is exactly what China would expect from India, while it operates in Southeast Asia. Additionally the hope is that with Chinese companies investing in India, there might be business pressure on Beijing to be more aware of infrastructure projects in territories sensitive in India, such as Arunachal Pradesh. While it will take a while for the two nations to break up their decades-old boundary issues, India should hold on to its *Act East policy* to deepen links with rural areas in China's periphery.

This will be the initiatal step towards getting Beijing to be alert of its own activities in India's neighbourhood.[25] To conclude, it may be said that India's Look East Policy has two dimensions. First is the External dimension, which essentially concerns relations of India as a whole with ASEAN (comprising Myanmar, Thailand, Cambodia, Laos, Malaysia, Singapore, Indonesia, Brunei, Vietnam and the Philippines) and East Asia which includes China, Japan and South Korea. The second dimension, which is the internal angle, is about development of Northeast India that makes it a viable gateway for the rest of India to ASEAN and East Asia.

There are several issues that need to be addressed in order to make "Act East" a success: First, India needs to "Act East" from *within*, i.e., in its northeastern region. Connectivity between the Northeast and other Indian states is still incomplete. While Myanmar is India's gateway to Southeast Asia, India's Northeast is its gateway to Myanmar. A major bottleneck in that regard is that even capitals of the northeastern states are not completely connected through road, rail, and air with one another and the rest of India. Guwahati and Kolkata are the only common links to northeastern cities. With such components missing within India, lack of connectivity with Southeast Asian countries becomes even more difficult. Connectivity with Southeast Asia can be realised only after intra-regional connectivity is ensured inside India.

Secondly, infrastructure development is an important component of the "Act East Policy." In this regard, India and the Southeast Asian countries have initiated several projects; however, implementation has been very slow. For instance, the Chennai-Dawei Sea Port Project is still in the initial stages. So is the India-Myanmar-Thailand trilateral highway.[26] The government has recently extended the project deadline from 2016 to 2018. Another major project to boost the connectivity between India and Southeast Asia is the Kaladan Multi-Modal Transit Transport Project. Once fully operational, it will link the Indian city of Kolkata to Sittwe port in Myanmar and will be extended up to the Indian state of Mizoram.[27] Maritime connectivity with Indonesia could further contribute to India's connectivity plans. This is important as Indonesia's Aceh province is less than 90 miles away from India's southernmost islands. Thirdly, people-to-people connectivity lies at the core of the "Act East Policy." Nalanda International University[28] and Buddhist tourist circuit can contribute immensely to Act East, provided the projects are implemented with rigour. Fourthly, despite improved economic stature at the international level, India has been consistently denied Asia-Pacific Economic Cooperation (APEC) membership, which does not augur well. From India's side, there is a need to persuade ASEAN member states to push for its membership. Strategists view that it is the "right time" for India to join the APEC bloc and become fully integrated into the global economy. Furthermore, India has to strive hard to gain a key position in the newly established BRICS[29] Bank.

Though "Act East" seems to be providing the necessary thrust to India's eastward engagement, India has to quit sitting on the fence on issues of strategic importance for the neighbourhood. Joint defence production and collaboration in defence Research & Development would help India firm up its capacities and also find lasting partnerships in the area. Indonesia, Japan, Singapore, and Vietnam are potential collaborators in that area. Robust people-to-people contacts and solid military and economic conflict with the region are the key to India's aim to turn a benign force of consequence. It is significant to realise that "Act East" does not entail getting into fights and oppositions; it entails creating an enabling environment for peace and prosperity.

Notes

A special Lecture was organised by the Jadavpur Association of International Relations (JAIR) on February 28, 2015, delivered by Ambassador Pinak Ranjan Chakravarty in collaboration with the Ministry of External Affairs, Governmet of India under this project.

A lecture Programme was organised on India's Act East Policy on March 21, 2015, delivered by Shri Rajeev Bhattacharjee, Renowned Journalist from Guwahati and Suraj L. Singh, Faculty D. M. College of Arts, Manipur at Observer Research Foundation under this project.

All the three lectures eventually helped us to get the government, civil society as well as theoretical conceptualisations of India's Look East-Act East Policy.

Notes

1. Chinglen Maisnam, "India's 'Act East' policy and North East," available at: http://www.manipurtimes.com/news-article/the-peoples-chronicle-article/item/16741-india-s-act-east-policy-north-east (retrieved on May 22, 2015).
2. C. Raja Mohan, "Not So Easy to Act East," *Indian Express*, November, 22, 2014.
3. Ibid.

4. For details refer the Lecture delivered by Ambassador Pinak Ranjan Chakravarty, Former Secretary, East, Ministry of External Affairs, Government of India, on the occasion of the Distinguished Lecture Programme organised by the Jadavpur Association of International Relations (JAIR) on February 28, 2015 at Ramakrishna Mission Institute of Culture, Kolkata.
5. Ibid.
6. "Obama's 'lead from behind' security strategy will plague America for decades," available at: http://www.latimes.com/opinion/op-ed/la-oe-0210-bolton-obama-national-security-strategy-20150210-story.html (retrieved on February 9, 2015).
7. India's Look East Policy dates back to the early 1990s when India, under the premiership of P. V. Narasimha Rao, had declared the "New Economic Policy" for the country with Dr. Manmohan Singh as the then Finance Minister of India. The phrase "Look East" actually denotes India's policies towards the Southeast Asian countries like Malaysia, Indonesia, Singapore, Myanmar, Brunei Darussalam, the Philippines, Thailand, Vietnam, Laos, Cambodia, etc. However, emphasis is also being given to East Asian countries like China, Japan and others. The process was accelerated further during the premiership of Atal Behari Vajpayee when India came much closer to the ASEAN (Association of Southeast Asian Nations), and finally when Dr. Manmohan Singh became the Prime Minister, emphasis was given not only to the "Look East" but also towards the "Look West" policy where the main focus was on the countries of the Middle East. At present Prime Minister Narendra Modi has focused on the concept of "Act East Policy" which is evident from the recent speeches of Sushma Swaraj, India's Minister of External Affairs, and also from Modi's foreign tours, especially to Myanmar.
8. For details refer to Anindita Malas, "The Journey from 'Look East' to 'Act East': A Critical Analysis of India's Look East Policy in Modern Times with special Reference to the Changes in the Governmental Set-ups," in Imankalyan Lahiri and Pahi Saikia (eds.), *North East in India's Look East: Issues and Opportunities* (New Delhi: Bharti Publications, 2015), pp. 201-13.
9. "From 'Look East' to 'Act East'—India shifts focus," http://www.dw.de/from-look-east-to-act-east-india-shifts-focus/a-18141462 downloaded on December 19, 2014 at 1.20 p.m. IST.
10. For details refer to Pinak Ranjan Chakravarty, n. 4.
11. http://www.mea.gov.in/distinguished-lectures-detail.htm?209 retrieved on May 20, 2015.
12. "Act East Policy starts with Bangladesh: PM Modi," *Business Standard*, December 19, 2014, New Delhi.
13. Danielle Rajendram, *India's new Asia-Pacific strategy: Modi acts East*, Lowy Institute.
14. Indo-Asian News Service (IANS), "India Needs Policy to Look East, Link West: Narendra Modi," *Deccan Herald*, September 25, 2014, available at: http://www.deccanherald.com/content/432698/india-needs-policy-look-east.html.
15. Pinak Ranjan Chakravarty, n. 4.
16. Chinglen Maisnam, "India's 'Act East' policy and North East," *The Manipur Times*, June 2, 2015.
17. Chinglen Maisnam, "India's 'Act East' policy and North East," ...
18. Namrata Goswami,"Bring Forth the North East," *The Hindu*, May 16, 2015.
19. For details refer to http://www.livemint.com/Opinion/tV4AlHMD3ZF39uYaLNPlwI/Bangladesh-ties-Narendra-Modi-needs-to-do-more.html (retrieved on June 7, 2015).
20. "Kolkata-Agartala bus service via Dhaka flagged off," *The Times of India*, June 7, 2015.
21. Pinak Ranjan Chakravarty, n. 4.

22. May 14, 2015-May 16, 2015.
23. China has recently justified as "goodwill" gesture its policy of issuing stapled visas to residents of Arunachal Pradesh, saying such a policy does not "undermine" the positions of both India and China which have disputes over big parts of that area. India has been protesting, maintaining that it does not recognise such visas. China claims that the state is "disputed," even as India continues to denounce the stance.
24. One Belt, One Road (Chinese: 一带一路; pinyin: Yídài yílù), also known as the Belt and Road Initiative; abbreviated OBOR) is a development strategy and framework, proposed by People's Republic of China that focuses on connectivity and cooperation among countries primarily in Eurasia, which consists of two main components, the land-based "Silk Road Economic Belt" (SREB) and ocean-going "Maritime Silk Road" (MSR). The strategy underlines China's push to take a bigger role in global affairs, and its need to export China's production capacity in areas of overproduction such as steel manufacturing.
25. Jhinuk Chowdhury, "How 'Act East' Can Be India's Key To Managing China," available at: http://www.huffingtonpost.in/jhinuk-chowdhury/can-act-east-be-indias-ke_b_7418840.html (retrieved on July 15, 2015).
26. Moe Thuzar, Rahul Mishra, Francis Hutchinson, Tin Maung, Maung Than, and Termsak Chalermpalanupap, "Connecting South and Southeast Asia: Implementation Challenges and Coordination Arrangements," ADBI Working Paper Series, Asian Development Bank Institute, no. 501, September 2014.
27. Ibid.
28. Nalanda University (also known as Nalanda International University) is a newly established university located in Rajgir, near Nalanda, Bihar, India. The University, created as a revival of an ancient centre of learning at Nalanda, began its first academic session on September 1, 2014, with 15 students including five women. Initially set up in temporary facilities in Rajgir, a modern campus is expected to be finished by 2020. Japan and Singapore are financing the construction work, with contributions totalling around US$ 100 million.
29. BRICS is the acronym for an association of five major emerging national economies: Brazil, Russia, India, China and South Africa. The grouping was originally known as "BRIC" before the inclusion of South Africa in 2010. The BRICS members are all developing or newly industrialised countries, but they are distinguished by their large, fast-growing economies and significant influence on regional and global affairs; all five are G-20 members. Since 2010, the BRICS nations have met annually at formal summits. Russia currently holds the chair of the BRICS group, and will host the group's seventh summit in July 2015.

3

MYANMAR: INDIA'S GATEWAY TO SOUTHEAST ASIA—A CASE STUDY OF MOREH-TAMU BORDER TRADE: TRANSFORMING CONNECTIVITY?

Introduction

Myanmar is the gateway to Southeast Asia. India-Myanmar[1] relations are rooted in shared historical, ethnic, cultural and religious ties. As the land of Lord Buddha, India is a country of pilgrimage for the people of Myanmar. Geographical proximity has also helped develop and sustain cordial relations and facilitated people-to-people contact. India and Myanmar share a long land border of over 1,600 km and a maritime boundary in the Bay of Bengal. A large population of Indian origin (according to some estimates, about 2.5 million) lives in Myanmar. India and Myanmar relations have stood the test of time. India and Myanmar signed a Treaty of Friendship in 1951. The visit of Prime Minister Rajiv Gandhi in 1987 laid the foundations for a stronger relationship between India and Myanmar. A number of agreements for enhancing bilateral cooperation have been signed between the two countries. Institutional mechanisms for facilitating regular dialogue on a range of issues of bilateral interest have also been established. Indian Consulate General in Mandalay was reopened in 2002 and the Consulate General of Myanmar was set up in Kolkata. India has been responsive to the needs of the friendly people of Myanmar and has been providing relief material and assistance.[2] India and Myanmar signed a border trade agreement in

1994 and have two operational border trade points: Moreh-Tamu and Zokhawthar-Rhi on the 1,643 km-long border. A third border trade point is proposed to be opened at Avakhung-Pansat/Somra. There is also the possibility of a fully developed Border Hat in the Changlang District of Arunachal Pradesh, which is known as the Pangsau Pass (Nampong). However, the two borders which are very important till date are:

- Moreh in Manipur State in India and Tamu in Myanmar (formally opened on April 12, 1995).
- Zokhawthar in Mizoram State in India and Rhi in Myanmar (began functioning on September 14, 2007).

Moreh-Tamu Border Trade

Of these two, the Moreh-Tamu border is the more important one because of the roadways as well as railways connectivity between India and Myanmar. Northeastern India shares a land border with Bangladesh, Bhutan, China, Myanmar and Nepal, and has agreements of overland trade with these countries through Land Customs Stations (LCS) notified under Section 7 of the Customs Act, 1962. While for trading through LCSs situated in Bangladesh and Bhutan border, there is a Free Trade Agreement (SAFTA), Border Trade Agreements have been entered into with China and Myanmar. Further, Border trade is different from trade through air, land or seaports as trade through ports involves clearance through customs and has a large volume. Border trade, in contrast, is "overland trade" by way of "exchange of commodities" from a bilaterally agreed list by people living along both sides of the international border. The present study attempts to examine India's border trade with Myanmar at Moreh in India and Tamu in Myanmar. The data has been mainly generated from secondary sources. It also includes some primary data collected during field visits at the study sites. The sources of the primary and secondary data includes the reports published by Asian Development Bank, Central Government publications, State

Government publications, joint report of the Confederation of Indian Industry (CII) and the Union of Myanmar Federation of Chambers of Commerce and Industry (UMFCCI), various journals, research papers, articles, books, PhD theses, various case studies, working papers, etc.

No economy in the world is perfectly independent. All countries are interdependent economically. In the absence of international trade, it will be difficult for a country to develop. Thus, international trade is regarded as the engine of growth of an economy. Border trade between India and Myanmar, which is a part of India's international trade, has great potential to influence economically the development of Northeastern India and Myanmar. To permit locally produced commodities to be traded as per prevailing customary practices on both sides of the India-Myanmar border, an agreement on border trade between India and Myanmar was signed on January 21, 1994 and operationalised on April 12, 1995. The Agreement envisages that border trade will take place through Customs Posts at Moreh in Manipur and Zokhawthar in Mizoram, corresponding to Tamu and Rhi in Myanmar.

Forty items are permitted for border trade between India and Myanmar, with 5% duty. Presently, most of the border trade takes place only through the Moreh Post.

During this study, a visit has been made to Moreh and Tamu to see the potential of the Moreh-Tamu trade point and to analyse how this trade relationship would improve the living conditions of the stakeholders of the Northeastern States. The objective of this field trip in mid-January 2015 was to analyse how far India is ready to take up the challenges of a free border trade. The Moreh-Tamu border is one of the most important borders India shares with Myanmar. This border could be used further to give full access to Indian citizens proceeding to Myanmar and vice versa by making it a vital point of entry for international travellers, travelling either to India or Myanmar. It would help both countries to improve cross-border trade, if it is successfully implemented. The Imphal-Mandalay bus service is the most talked about proposed bus route in recent years to connect India and Myanmar in a simplified and cost-effective way. Moreh is a small border town located in the Chandel District of Manipur. This particular town shares its border with a small town known as Tamu located in the Sagine division of Myanmar. It is important to note that Manipur is gradually becoming a "hotspot" under Look East Policy in regard to India's connectivity with Southeast Asian Nations. Moreh is essentially an International border town on the national highway number 39 (now AH-1). This roadway is one of the major road linkages between India and Myanmar, and ends at the Indo-Myanmar Friendship road leading towards the Asian Highway-1 on Myanmar's side. The distance between Imphal to Moreh is 110 kilometres. The landscape is mostly mountainous. However, since suspicion and poor road conditions are vital problems in the Indian state of Manipur, it takes nearly 6 to 7 hours to cover 110 kilometres to reach Moreh. There are multiple authorities who are responsible for control of these check posts. They are:

- Customs Preventive Force, Moreh
- Moreh Police Gate, Moreh
- 24 Assam Rifles, Khudengthabi
- 165 G-coy, Assam Regiment, Lokchao
- Tengnoupal Police Station, Tengnoupal
- 18 Assam Rifles, Tengnoupal
- 44 Assam Rifles, Bongyang
- Police Outpost, Pallel
- Pallel customs.

The check points controlled by the armed forces are many. The major check points where the checking takes place are as follows:

- Bongyang Check Point
- Tengnoupal Check Post
- Khudengthabi Check Post

The first check post is at Bongyang. This check post is under the 20 Assam Rifles Force. The second check post is located in the Tengnoupal; a subdivision headquarters of the Chandel District. This check post is under the 26th sector of the 24 Assam Rifles Force. Here the checking mechanism is quite slow as they permit only one car at a time. This reduces the pace of movement of traffic. It is important for India to develop security check mechanisms. 24 Assam Riffles also control the Khudengthabi check post.

Picture 3.1: The Lok Chaw Bridge

Besides, one has to cross the Lok Chaw Bridge which is not well maintained and only one car can cross it at a time. Sometimes vehicles need to wait a long time to cross this bridge. Travellers face huge problems at times when this bridge is under repair and renovation. In such situations it may take one and a half hours or even two hours to cross the bridge. Traffic coming from Moreh or from Imphal stands in a line to cross this bridge, often leading to commotion and traffic jams. This does not portray a good image of India for those coming from other countries. We need to keep in mind that this bridge falls on the way leading to Asian Highway No. 1. Importantly, the condition of the road from Imphal to Bongyang, the place where the road way enters its hilly section, needs to be improved. However, once this road enters the hills, its condition is much better. Traffic moves quite smoothly in the hilly section of NH 39. But the security check posts essentially delay the movement of traffic, and it is necessary to improve the security check mechanisms on the Indian side. India has to take into account that this particular road is an integral part of international road linkage, and therefore should be improved from all aspects, including the delayed security checks by military personnel.

After crossing the Lok Chaw Bridge the traffic movement is much smoother as the road now is well maintained. The road crossing the Chandel District of Manipur reaches Moreh having a last security check post as Khudengthabi. Traffic gets stuck at this particular point, as one vehicle is checked at a time, which makes movement very slow. Here the search mechanisms are conventional and traditional. It is difficult for travellers to reopen their bags each and every time while travelling on this road. Government of India urgently needs to look into this matter. X-ray baggage checking system, or even better technologies, can be used as this will not only be convenient for the travellers and the army, but will also bring about transparency and cleanliness in the checking process. This check point has X-ray check machines only for ladies handbags. Cars coming from Imphal or Moreh need to wait for a long time to get the security checks done. All the cars are searched and the travellers need to open up all their luggage and belongings and everyone needs to cross this check point on foot. The question however remains why, in Indian territory, an Indian citizen must cross this check point on foot. Government must have an improved mechanism to conduct these checks. Khudengthabi check post is the gateway to Moreh.

Picture 3.2: Moreh: The town of uncertainty?

On reaching Moreh, one sees some peculiar and exotic features. Being a small but very important town, commercially as well as from diplomatic aspects, it does not have any proper hotels and restaurants for the International travellers, apart from one government lodge. The local population, especially the women folk, provides minimal facilities of boarding and lodging. Manipur is known to be a dry state but the people have a free and open access to liquor. Moreh is a border town where people from the other side, that is, Myanmar, have access to it. But the town does not provide a positive picture of India to international visitors. This is not only because of the lack of infrastructure, but also due to the lack of cleanliness. With permission from the Home Department, one can go to Tamu, the Myanmarese village town, by crossing the International Gate No. 1 with their own vehicle. The permit is normally given for a day visit. Travellers are allowed to cross the Indo-Myanmar friendship bridge at the gate number 1 only till 6 pm. The only requirement to cross this bridge is an immigration letter from the customs house. Once this bridge is crossed travellers get access to the Asian Highway no. 1, and once travellers enter Tamu in Myanmar, they see a very different picture. In contrast to that of India, the Myanmarese army do not open the bags of each and every person. They only check the immigration letter. Most astonishingly, Tamu though being a very small town in the Sagine division of Myanmar, it is extremely clean, well maintained and decorated. Undoubtedly the Myanmarese army is working well to keep this border town clean. Unlike Moreh, Tamu has small eateries as well as big restaurants. There are big hotels and shops where almost everything is available. Shopkeepers readily accept Indian Rupees from Indians, and this is helping Myanmar to increase their foreign exchange reserves, although the method is a direct one. The Tamu market at Gate No. 2 provides a huge variety of products, ranging from vegetables to electronic goods, which the Indian market at Moreh does not provide. This is one of the main reasons behind people's preference to go to Tamu for trading purposes. Indians are unable to visit the interiors of Tamu as the Indian insurgent groups sheltered in Myanmar prohibit such movement. But, on the whole, Tamu shows a much better picture of Myanmar than that shown by Moreh of India. However, to facilitate limited movement of hill tribes residing along the Indo-Myanmar border, the Governments of India and Myanmar have permitted entry of such persons residing within 16 km of the international border with only permits but without visas, under certain terms and conditions. Local nationals of both sides can stay in the other country for three days within 16 km on either side.[3] Tamu, unlike Moreh, is well maintained and has gradually developed an integrated marketplace acceptable to international visitors. The customs house or the army people do not even maintain their own compound. Good hotels and restaurants are available for international travellers in Tamu. Before the signing of the Indo-Myanmar Border Trade Agreement, there was traditional exchange of goods between the people living along both sides of the border. The Kachins in Myanmar-China border, the Karens in Myanmar-Thailand border, the Rohingyas in Myanmar-Bangladesh and the Tamil Chettiars, and Nagas and the Kuki, Chin and Mizo in India-Myanmar border have been carrying on border trade. Hill tribals inhabiting the border areas along the India-Myanmar border enjoyed the facility of free movement up to 40 km on either side on the entire length of 1,643 km, the reason being that they had close affinity and cultural and economic ties. They enjoyed this facility until 1968 when

Government of India unilaterally introduced a permit system to check entry of undesirable elements and insurgents.[4] From 1948 to 1962 there was a friendly and cordial relationship between the two countries, but there was a strained relationship from 1962 to 1992-1993. From 1993 onwards India reversed its stance with a more realistic and pragmatic policy and started engaging the military regime. Since then, relations have been growing steadily and there has been all-round progress in political, economic and military relations as well as cooperation in technology, HRD, infrastructure, education, health care and other fields.

Picture 3.3: Indo-Myanmar Friendship Gate, at Gate No. 2.

There is also a Gate No. 2, and on the other side of the Road there is the Tamu marketplace. The goods are extremely cheap and almost all goods are made in China. The Myanmarese market has been taken over by Chinese goods. On the other hand, the Indian side is extremely poor in its infrastructure and no good market is found. There are scattered shops on the Indian side, and the concept of full-fledged market is absent, as compared to the Myanmarese side. The Indo-Myanmar Friendship Gate located here is known as the gateway to Southeast Asia. Indo-Myanmar Friendship Gate is located in Moreh town within Chandel district in the Indian state of Manipur. It is an important trade point in India on the border with Myanmar. By the side of Gate No. 1 is the Indo-Myanmar Friendship Bridge which connects India to Kalewa in Myanmar's Sagaing Division. The highway on the Myanmar side is intended to run up to Mandalay. Indian planners hope the rail link to Moreh will eventually be connected to the Myanmar railway system, allowing onward connectivity to Thailand and China, thus leading to a future vision of the Trans-Asian Railways that will enable containers from Singapore, China, Vietnam, Cambodia, India, Bangladesh, Myanmar, Thailand and Korea to travel overland by train to Europe. It is also called India's Gateway to Southeast Asia. The Indian and Myanmar delegates also started the survey work for Imphal-Mandalay bus service recently. The joint team travelled up to Mandalay via Yargyi in Myanmar from India. The Myanmar team was led by U San Aung, Director General of Railways, U Than Toe Aung, U Kyaw Kyaw, U Aung Soe, U Kyaw Thu Zaw, Superintendent Engineers of Sagaing Region, Public Works Department, Ministry of Construction. The Indian team was led by an Official of the Ministry of External Affairs and the engineers from the Ministry of Roads and Transport, Government of India.[5]

Picture 3.4: Indo-Myanmar Bridge near Gate No. 1 (Asian High Way 1)

On the Indo-Myanmar border, border trade at concessional rates and with certain conditions is permissible for 40 bilaterally agreed items. In addition, normal trade is also permitted. Directorate General of Foreign Trade (DGFT), Ministry of Commerce, Government of India has clarified that "normal trade" in all other commodities between the two countries through Land Customs Station at Moreh is also permitted subject to payment of customs duties as applicable on international trade with any other country of the world.[6] Thus, while border trade is carried out at a concessional duty of 5% on 40 identified items, normal/MFN trade is also permitted in Moreh and Zokhawthar. The Indo-Myanmar Border trade includes 40 items, shown in the Figure 3.1:

Figure 3.1: Indo-Myanmar Border Trade Items (Total 40 items)

Sl. No.	Old items (DGFT Public Notice No. 289 (PN) /92-97 dated April 10, 1995)	Sl. No.	Additional items (DGFT Public Notice No. 106 (RE-2008)/2004-2009 dated November 7, 2008)
1.	Mustard/rape seeds	23.	Bicycle spare parts
2.	Pulses and beans	24.	Life-saving drugs
3.	Fresh vegetables	25.	Fertilisers
4.	Fruits	26.	Insecticides
5.	Garlic	27.	Cotton fabrics
6.	Onion	28.	Stainless steel utensils
7.	Chillies	29.	Menthol
8.	Spices (excluding nutmeg, mace, cloves and cassia)	30.	Agarbatti
9.	Bamboo	31.	Spices
10.	Minor forest produce (excluding teak)	32.	Cosmetics
11.	Betel nuts and leaves	33.	Leather footwear
12.	Food items for local consumption	34.	Paints and varnishes
13.	Tobacco	35.	Sugar and salt
14.	Tomato	36.	Mosquito Coils
15.	Reed broom	37.	Bulbs
16.	Sesame	38.	Blades
17.	Resin	39.	X-ray paper and Photo paper
18.	Coriander seeds	40.	Imitation jewellery
19.	Soya bean		
20.	Roasted sunflower seeds		
21.	Katha		
22.	Ginger		

Note: India has notified 22 additional items including agricultural tools, bicycles, coal and garments in the list of items for border trade with Myanmar. In a notification, the Directorate General of Foreign Trade (DGFT) said the existing arrangements for import/export of items under Indo-Myanmar Border have been revised and 22 new items have been added to the existing list of 40 tradable items, taking the number of total tradable items to 62 for border trade. The other new items are: 1. Agricultural machinery/equipment/tools, 2. Bicycles, 3. Bleaching powder, 4. Coal, 5. Edible oil, 6. Electrical & electric appliances, 7. Fabricated steel products, 8. Garments/readymade garments/cloth, 9. Handloom and handicrafts items, 10. Hardware/ minor construction materials and electrical fittings, 11. Lime, 12. Medicines, 13. Milk powder, tea, edible oil, beverages, 14. Motorcycles & Motorcycle spare parts, 15. Other items such as electronic/musical instruments, stationary items, torchlight, 16. Plastic items: water tank, buckets, chairs, plastic pipes and briefcases, 17. Rice, wheat, maize, millets & oats, 18. Scented tobacco, 19. Semi-precious stones, 20. Sewing machines, 21. Textile fabrics, 22. Three wheelers/cars below 1,000 C.C. (Public Notice No. 30 (RE-2012)/2009-2014, New Delhi, dated the 16th November 2012)

Figure 3.2: Cross-Border Trade Through Moreh

India-Myanmar Trade			
	2009-10	**2010-11**	**% growth**
Myanmar	207.97	334.42	60.81
(% Share)	-0.11	-0.133	
India's total export	178,751.43	251,135.89 40.49	
($ million)			

Source: Ministry of Commerce, Government of India, 2012.

However, it is also important to see the trade figures in other Land Customs Stations of India-Myanmar land border.

Table 3.3: India-Myanmar Border Trade (official figures)

Name of Land Customs Station	Exports (Rs. lakhs)				Imports (Rs. lakhs)				Main items of Export	Main items of Import
Moreh	2009-10	2010-11	2011-12	2012-13	2009-10	2010-11	2011-12	2012-13	Cumin seed & Soyabari	Betel nut & Ginger
	831	380	137	2055	831	380	137	2055		
Zokhawthar	2009-10	2010-11	2011-12	2012-13	2009-10	2010-11	2011-12	2012-13	Cumin	Betel nut
	0.60	4.34	22.27 Nil	0.60	Nil	2.10	1.8			
Nampong	**No Trade**									

Source: Central Board of Excise and Customs (CBEC).

It is important to discuss here that there are certain strategic rationale which determine the contours of Indo-Myanmar relations. These are as follows:

- Myanmar is located at the tri-junction of East Asia, South Asia and Southeast Asia.
- Myanmar is the second largest of India's neighbours, and the largest on the eastern flank.
- Myanmar provides the Eastern littoral of the Bay of Bengal. An unfriendly Myanmar hosting foreign naval presence would pose a threat to Indian security.
- Myanmar has a big border with China in the North, contiguous with the Sino-Indian disputed border, which has many implications.
- India has both a land border (1,643 km) and a maritime boundary with Myanmar in the Bay of Bengal, four Indian states (Arunachal Pradesh, Nagaland, Manipur and Mizoram) border Myanmar (Kachin and Chin states and Sagaing Division)
- China can gain access to Indian Ocean through Myanmar.

Problems behind the Border Trade

Myanmar is India's gateway to ASEAN as it is the only country of this grouping which has a land and maritime boundary with India. With India becoming a summit level partner of ASEAN and a member of the East Asia Summit, improved relations with Myanmar will be beneficial in many respects. Besides, Myanmar and India are members of subregional groupings such as BIMSTEC and Mekong Ganga Cooperation. On the other hand, China has raised its economic profile in Southeast Asia, particularly in Myanmar, despite the sanctions imposed by the West. India should not be left behind especially in view of the large oil and gas resources available in Myanmar which are much needed by India. So it is important for India to develop this border trade to establish further relationship with Myanmar. It is important to note here that UBI, Moreh branch and Myanmar Economic Bank at Tamu, Myanmar are the two banks on both sides which are designated and authorised to enable normal trade under the letter of credit system.

Picture 3.4: Photo taken from the Indian Side to the Myanmar Side: The Porous Border?

However, there are certain security considerations which are not giving full scope to this Indo-Myanmar Border trade. These are:

1. **Insurgency in the Border Areas**

Some of the insurgent groups have established camps in Myanmar and operate from Myanmarese territory. Indian insurgent groups have taken refuge in the Tamu area of Myanmar, one of which is Kangleipak Communist Party (KCP), a Manipuri insurgent group. Pha Lon Market located in Tamu includes more than 1,000 shops that sell basic commodities, rice and clothing, often to Indian traders who bring the goods back to India's Manipur State via the Tamu-Moreh border highway. Medicine, dyes and cotton are often brought to Burma from India. The Indian government and Indian media say Manipuri insurgencies, including the KCP, operate in Tamu and other areas in northwest Burma. But the Burmese government has said that these groups are not allowed to operate on Burmese soil.[7] During my field visit to the area, my friend, who is a teacher in one of the government colleges of Manipur, informed me that there is no definite proof that the Myanmarese government is giving refuge to Indian insurgents, but it is an open secret that Indian insurgent groups do have their base in this area. During our visit to Tamu, my Manipuri friends, advised us not to move further outside the market since there is always a threat from the insurgent groups for the Indians visiting the area. My friends advised us not to disclose our identity during our visit to Tamu.

2. Smuggling of Arms (by Land and Sea)

The illegal arms trade takes place on the Moreh-Tamu Border. Most of the illegal arms are coming from the Yunnan province of China and reaches the Moreh Border through Tamu. Moreh-Tamu has been rated as a high-intensity centre of illegal trade. The cost of illegal arms is around Rs. 2 lakhs to Rs. 5 lakhs. The insurgent groups in the Northeast had been procuring arms through "smugglers" based in China's Yunnan province, Myanmar and Southeast Asian countries. Weapons in small consignments were then transported either via Myanmar or Bangladesh to India. India had raised its concern with China, Myanmar and Bangladesh from time to time, through diplomatic channels, about the reported smuggling of arms through their territories. But no final agreements have been reached so far. To check smuggling across the Indo-Myanmar border, a Memorandum of Understanding was signed between India and Myanmar in January 1994, for maintenance of peace and tranquillity in border areas. The Central government has stepped up vigilance and surveillance along the border. The security forces along the border have been suitably sensitised regarding arms smuggling by insurgents, and regular patrolling along the border areas is being carried out. But corruption has grasped the region and a strong vigilance is required to control the situation.

3. Drug Trafficking and Narco-Terrorism

Drug trafficking and nacro-terrorism are the other two problems of the Moreh-Tamu border. This route is also notorious for drug trafficking. According to United Nations Office on Drugs and Crime, medicines are smuggled from Kunming into Myanmar and then proceed from Monywa near Mandalay to Tamu/Moreh on the Indian border. The report says that from here the consignments go to exporters in Maharashtra, Gujarat and Tamil Nadu.

On the other hand Indo-Myanmar border trade has certain restrictions. These may include:

1. Restriction on the Import of Timber

The import of Myanmar timber is allowed through every post of India except through Moreh. There is a tremendous potential for timber imports from Myanmar as the location of Moreh is in the vicinity of the vast timber producing areas of Myanmar. Scarcity of timber in our own country holds a natural advantage for trading in Myanmar timber. As per the decision of High Powered Committee's meeting held on June 19, 2003, import of timber from Myanmar was allowed only under the condition that it would be used for local consumption and would not be allowed to be moved outside Manipur.

2. Collection of Taxes

Collection of sales tax, forest royalty and other taxes on import of goods by the state government of Manipur has added to the tax burden of Indian importers. High transportation cost and such taxes reduce the cost-effectiveness of the trade.

3. Illegal Collection of Taxes

The main vehicles plying on this national highway from Imphal to Moreh are Buses, Tata Sumos, Maruti Vans and Trucks for the purpose of transportation of goods and passengers. So many underground organisations are collecting illegal taxes from these vehicles. It is important to note here that as per the information collected, commercial vehicles plying from Imphal to Moreh, pay heavy illegal taxes to different underground organisations of the state, and the government has not yet taken any appropriate steps to stop this.

4. Community Crises and Law and Order Problem of Moreh Town

Moreh town is a place of different communities with Kukis making up the highest number of the population. There were community crises between Kukis and Tamils and Kukis and Meiteis. In such a situation, it is very difficult to have a free and smooth trade. In addition to this, there are frequent bandhs and blockades in Moreh town as well as on the highway connecting Imphal to Moreh.

Picture 3.5: Tamu: Uncertainty and Beyond?

5. Tamu, a Place with Uncertainty

Tamu remains a place of uncertainty. There is always confusion amongst the traders regarding their security. Indian insurgent groups taking refuge in the Tamu area is a common factor. In a recent incident, the bodies of Sanvendar Singh (30) from Uttar Pradesh and Daljeet Singh (33) from Maharashtra, who went missing after entering Myanmar's Tamu district, were found inside a jungle near Jangnomphai village about 45 km from Moreh police station, after ten days. In a free trade regime, it is expected that both countries should ensure protection of traders' lives within their respective territories.

6. Lack of Infrastructural Facilities for International/Border Trade

With a weighbridge, a Trade Centre building, and a two-lane road in poor condition, it is difficult for the cross-border trade between the two countries to prosper. For roads, at least, the basic infrastructure of trade already exists. Manipur connects to mainland India via two major highways: National Highway 102 (NH-102) is the extension of AH-1; it goes northwards into central Assam, and National Highway 37 (NH-37) runs westwards into southern Assam. These two highways are essential not just for overland trade to Myanmar, but also for providing Manipur with the rice, petrol, cement, and other basic commodities which the state imports from other parts of India. However, both highways are plagued by shoddy construction, especially NH-37: Even in the dry season, travelling the 220 km from Imphal to Jiribam on Manipur's western border can take 13-14 hours. The border trading environment itself is characterised by a combination of weak basic infrastructure and byzantine bureaucratic procedures. A June 2014 report by Manipur-based Hueiyen News Service notes that the town struggles to guarantee five hours power daily—a major obstacle to state government plans for establishing a cold storage centre, a must-have for high-volume trade in a host of food products. In 2006, central government authorities approved the development of an Integrated Check Post (ICP) at Moreh—a single complex for border management authorities, intended to improve inter-agency coordination. Construction is currently halted on account of Myanmar's claims, announced in December 2013, that the ICP site lies on its territory. In the meantime, a 2011 report on border infrastructure at Moreh suggested that maintenance of current customs facilities had dropped off since ICP development began. Such deficits work against the sort of professional trading operations that Delhi policymakers seek to encourage. In fact, the vast majority of Moreh's trade goes through informal and illegal channels. Official statistics for these channels do not exist; but estimates I have heard—both publicly available (as in these reports) and in my own conversations with experts in Manipur—indicate that the annual volumes moving through each of these channels today stands somewhere in the billions to tens of billions of rupees, far above the hundreds of millions of rupees in annual formal trade.[8]

7. **Exchange Rate of Currencies—Kyat and Indian Rupee**

Myanmar's currency is the Kyat. It must be one of the most unstable currencies in the world. At present, in the market, it sells at the rate of Rs. 100 to Kyat 3,100. In the year 2005, the rate was Rs. 100 to Kyat 2,000. In the year 2000-1, it was Rs. 100 to Kyat 750 and a few years earlier, it was Rs. 100 to Kyat 350. But, officially, when we see the exchange rate between the US Dollar and Kyat and the US Dollar and Indian Rupee, the Kyat has a higher value. So, Indian traders do not prefer to trade legally and through banks.

Though there are a number of stumbling blocks in the way of the border trade between India and Myanmar, in the year 2006-7, there was a huge increase in the volume of trade through Moreh. There is enough potential for further growth of trade between the two countries. Government of India has taken up certain initiatives to bring further increase in the trade. But, the important thing is that the state government should also frame strategic industrial and economic policies so that our state can be benefited from this cross-border trade.

Steps should be taken to block illegal trade, and the state police and security forces should be sincere and honest in performing their duties. Special emphasis should be given towards the development of quality, skilful and standardised human resources in the state. As pointed out earlier, both legal and "informal" trade is carried on between Manipur and Myanmar, especially in the border town of Moreh[9] on the Indian side, and Tamu on the Myanmar side. The value of informal border trade transacted through Moreh is estimated at Rs. 2,000 crores a year.[10] The development of Moreh border trade is set to expand several fold and contribute to the growth of Manipur's economy in the near future. It may well become the nodal point for international trade links with the rest of the East and Southeast Asian countries. A large number of Muslims and others from mainland India were also engaged in this border trade. There is growing competition among different communities living in the border areas for acquiring control over trade. This has led to a conflict between the Nagas and the Kukis, and between the Tamils and the Kukis in Moreh. Violent clashes occurred between the Nagas and the Kukis in 1993. Again, in 1995, there were ethnic clashes between the Kukis and the Tamils due to the Kuki militants' attempt to impose heavy taxes on the Tamil business community in this area. Although roadways are the main channel for border trade in Manipur, waterways through the Barak valley in the southernmost subdivision of Tipaimukh (Churachandpur district) were also used. The barter system is time-tested and is still practised. Exchanges other than the barter trade are transacted through the Indian Rupee and the Myanmar Kyat; the exchange rate is arrived at by mutual agreement between the traders every day. This is done through recognised local money changers. It is estimated that on an average trade valued at Rs. 50 crores is exchanged/converted every day at Moreh alone. A huge portion of this money is black money, which is one important reason why the border trade could not contribute much to Manipur's economy. With careful planning and execution this can change. However, it must not become a substitute for domestic, industrial and agricultural growth. Trade by itself may reduce Manipur (or Moreh) to a transition point between Asia and the rest of India, without catalysing growth. If this happens, only a few traders or trading corporations will benefit. Other illegal practices such as dumping might hamper industrial development in the region. Trade in primary commodities without value addition and processing will severely inhibit the potential advantages and result in unequal and unfair trade.

The state and Central Governments need to intervene to develop this area as an effective international trade centre. The main players actively engaged directly and indirectly in the Indo-Myanmar border trade is the traders, the underground workers, the police and the forest officials. It is reported that these groups form part of a strong network and as such regulating it will not be an easy task.

Existing Initiatives to Boost Trade and Commerce in the Northeast Area

- An empowered Committee under the chairmanship of the Commerce Secretary functions in the Department of Commerce to monitor and implement initiatives for the Northeast following the announcement in January 2000 of a specific set of measures for the development of this region, known as "PM's Action Plan for the Northeast."
- For creation of infrastructure under the Assistance to States for Infrastructure Development for Exports and other activities (ASIDE) Schemes, during 2004-5, an amount of Rs. 36 crores, constituting 10% of the outlay under the Scheme, was allocated by the Department of Commerce for the region.
- Land Customs Stations are gateways for the transit of goods, services and human beings between neighbouring countries. Among the border towns, four towns—Moreh, Sutarkandi, Dawki and Zokhawthar—were given priority for development. The Central Warehousing Corporation (CWC) has conducted a study of the infrastructure facilities required at Moreh (Manipur).

Some suggestions for strengthening trade ties within the Northeast and the bordering country Myanmar:

- Industrialisation must precede the opening up of trade.
- There is ample scope for the development of manufacturing/processing units for medicines, rubber goods, cycles and cycle parts, pharmaceuticals, edible oils, petroleum products, cement, cotton yarns, etc.
- Trade in simple daily use commodities (in headloads), often through barter, has been immediately beneficial to local people and must not be lost sight of in discussions around more substantive inter-country trade.
- A facilitative infrastructure needs to be developed in the Moreh-Tamu area by initiating steps for upgrading the existing network of roads and strengthening banking with facilities for currency exchange, etc.
- The border should not become merely a transit point for export and import of goods.

The local people should not be reduced to mere headload workers. Local industry like agro-processing, horticulture, textiles, etc., must be encouraged through the employment-led expansion of the regional market, replacement of outside products with local produce and servicing external demand. On the positive side, Prime Minister Manmohan Singh has also indicated that Moreh would be made a hub of cross-border trade with Myanmar. In October, during the visit of President of Myanmar, U Thein Sein, to India, both countries discussed the feasibility of cross-border road and rail networks. Manmohan Singh was reported to have discussed with U Thein Sein the possibility of a road linking Moreh-Mae Sot that would connect India and Thailand via Myanmar.

In October 2006, the Indian government had also proposed to build a railway line from Jiribam to Imphal and Moreh. This railway line is part of the Mekong-Ganga Cooperation Initiative. According to the assessment of Rites Limited, construction of a rail link between Jiribam-Imphal-Moreh would cost of Rs. 2,941.08 crores. Construction of a rail link would also be required in Myanmar between Tamu-Kalay-Segyi at a cost of Rs. 1,339.02 crores and rehabilitation of existing line from Segyi-Chaungu Myohaung at a cost of Rs. 283.959 crores. So far, the Indian Railways have only begun work on the Jiribam-Imphal line, expected to be completed by 2016.[11]

It is true that this area has changed a lot during the last two years. Insurgency in the region is getting limited. The fear amongst the common people is also getting reduced. Manipur's capital town, Imphal, is now more or less ready to take the challenge of border trade through Moreh. New hotels with facilities to international standards are coming up in Moreh. It is also true that Moreh may have long lost its former glory, but in Manipur the town still enjoys its reputation, made obvious by how the locals expand its name—Millions of Rupees Enter Here (Moreh). This reputation of Moreh for big money comes from the Southeast Asian trade, which traders here have been indulging in for decades, both legally and illegally. Trade is driven by a close-knit group of around 700 Tamil and another 15 Sikh and Marwari families who have the reputation of knowing Southeast Asia like the back of their hand. This select group of traders is able to successfully conduct trade with countries as far as Thailand, China and Vietnam.[12] Officially recorded trade between India and Myanmar through the border trade points of Moreh and Zokhawthar was only US$ 6.5 million in 2012-13 as per the Central Board of Excise and Customs (CBEC) figures. On the other hand, estimates of informal trade that takes place across the border are several times higher. Such a situation with a miniscule officially recorded border trade, accompanied by large unregulated informal trade, is fraught with security, health, safety and other risks and is certainly not sustainable if we are looking for accelerated trade expansion across the border as a means of bringing growth and economic development to this region. This needs correction at the earliest. Furthermore, Moreh could emerge as a support centre for trade promotion activities by having commodity exchanges, logistics servicing and warehousing facilities, and providing a transportation support hub. The emergence of such a modern township could also greatly contribute to removing the disincentive that officials (from customs, immigration, police or security) perceive to take up assignments at Moreh. Our personal impression during the visit to Moreh-Tamu is that, if Government of India really wants to improve this border area, infrastructural development in the Moreh area is a must, with enhanced security. Corruption must be eliminated. There are many incidents where Indian officials are involved in the illegal trade being conducted. The role of the military in the region must be monitored by the government. Too much power in the hands of the military may reduce the mission of the government in the region. It is expected that proper source of entertainment, shops, etc., are immediately required by the local stakeholders along with health security. Multi-facility super hospitals must be built in the border region. Restoration of democracy in Myanmar is one of the most important developments witnessed by Asia in the contemporary period. After a prolonged isolation, Myanmar has embarked on a path of political and economic reforms since 2011, paving the way for unlocking the country's large potential. India must take full advantage for the development of its Northeastern region.

Conclusion

It can be said here that if the purpose of any foreign bilateral policy is to encourage a change of course for the other, India's engagement of Myanmar has met with moderate, far from spectacular, success. In security terms, India can be assured that Myanmar has not become a "client state" of China, that formal links between the two countries' respective armed forces have matured, and cross-border cooperation on control of arms and drug trafficking is in place. On the significant subject of counter-insurgency cooperation, however, Myanmar gives all the right assurances but has neglected to implement. As long as Indian Insurgent Groups (IIGs) are able to find a safe haven across the border, New Delhi's ambitions to bring peace and evolution to its Northeast will remain unrealised. While China has been able to effectively pressure Myanmar to control its eastern border regions, the spoils to be had from border trade with the Northeast—one of the most underdeveloped areas in India—simply have not compared to those from China's thriving Yunnan Province.

Economically, India will be pleased with the steady growth in trade between the two lands, and with the expanding portfolio of investments it has been able to make in Myanmar's oil and gas sector. Nevertheless, the major prize of securing direct access to gas reserves and hydropower for electricity generation for the Northeast has so far eluded New Delhi largely due to conditions beyond its control. Alas, the lack of progress on the many visionary connectivity projects initiated by India cannot be blamed on third parties. Myanmar has not presented these projects a high priority so far, with only one project—the 160 km Moreh-Kalewa Road into Chin State—having been completed in 2001.

Myanmar's transition to democracy and a liberalised economy seemingly opens up tantalising opportunities for trade, investment and energy security for India. The scale of Myanmar's development needs will mean that India's ambitious Sittwe Port, Kaladan multi-modal highway, and trilateral highway projects are likely to be well defended by a prospective NLD government.

Increased border trade and infrastructure construction to connect Myanmar's economy to both India and ASEAN can only be seen as positive developments for the country's citizenry. But as the junta was keen to improve relations with India to maintain a degree of foreign policy autonomy from China, this can also be expected of the National League for Democracy (NLD). Indian companies too deliver an opportunity to capitalise on community concerns about Chinese investment by establishing a larger degree of societal duty and desire to ensure greater community benefit in the implementation of research tasks. Many obstacles, however, are yet to be overcome before an optimistic assessment about the prospects for India-Myanmar relations can be granted, even if the NLD takes power in 2015. Myanmar is likely to continue to be a safe haven for IIGs, given that the Tatmadaw has its own interests in leaving them to operate in the border districts. Moreover, the NLD does not look to cause a believable programme to add up to a political settlement with ethnic insurgent groups, and until a permanent peace is conveyed to the borderlands, IIGs will continue use that location. Economically, while the NLD has shown that it is committed to greater liberalisation, and expanding opportunities for trade and foreign investment, even where projects are unpopular, there is yet a long way to go to make the conditions for a real increase in relations between the two nations. It will take some time to improve the rule of law and tackle endemic corruption. Efforts must still be made to break the monopolies of military conglomerates and "cronies," to expose state-owned enterprises to competition, and to create open processes for the awarding of resource licences.[13] For Myanmar, it also made sense to develop deep relations with India. The two countries therefore must identify their strengths and requirements to work towards mutual benefit, and one of the important features is to improve border trade between India and Myanmar.

India's lack of capacity to become an influential trade and investment partner is driven by several factors, which include India's underdeveloped energy infrastructure, which limits New Delhi's capacity to transfer and distribute Myanmar's oil and natural gas in India; the reality that the two countries' common border is undeveloped, which contrasts with Myanmar's border with China; and bureaucratic hurdles and red tape that impede the cross-border trade and investment process.

India has every reason to hold close to Myanmar at this time, and to make as much progress as is possible on the trade and investment front. India's interest in integrating India's isolated Northeast with the rest of the country will continue to provide Indian officials with an incentive to deepen economic, political and military ties with Myanmar. Yet security dilemmas on both sides of the border constitute major concerns for Indian authorities. For example, the Buddhist orchestrated pogroms against Myanmar's Muslims have led to a radicalisation of some Muslims in the region, which threatens to result in retaliatory attacks against Buddhist institutions in India and other corners of South and Southeast Asia. The Naga community, situated on both sides of the border, will also remain a concern for both governments as the concept of "Nagalim" potentially threatens both states' territorial integrity.

From Myanmar's perspective, deeper ties with India can alleviate some of its own concerns about destabilising developments on its side of the edge, while also showing that the state can balance its partnership with China along with other regional players. Given Myanmar's economic and political dependence on Beijing, it should be anticipated that the government in Nay Pyi Taw will only practise so much, and with care. Even if Myanmar's relationship with China does not fundamentally shift (and we do not anticipate that it will), India—and other countries, such as the United States and Japan—offer Nay Pyi Taw greater leverage against Beijing by emphasising that Myanmar has other choices. Chinese officials consider the gradual evolution of economic, political and military relationships with India as a threat to Beijing's unique relationship with the land. Myanmar's government understands the value it offers to both India and China. India's security dilemmas and its interest in new sources of oil and natural gas will continue to drive its ambitions vis-à-vis Myanmar for the foreseeable future. At the same time, China's access to the Bay of Bengal via Myanmar, and the security of energy accessibility via its landlocked southern provinces, make Myanmar an important strategic partner for Beijing. Within this context, deepening ties between India and Myanmar will remain an issue for China.[14]

Irrespective of whether Myanmar completes its democratic transition or retreats to resume its previous exclusive status, its geostrategic significance and natural resources will continue to determine the balance of power in a region where Chinese and Indian interests intersect. China and India can indeed coexist in Myanmar, but China will hold a distinct advantage by virtue of its recent history, the nature of its military assistance, and its alignment of long-term interests with Nay Pyi Taw. Therefore, it is important for India to move prudently and to enhance land-to-land connectivity with Myanmar to enhance its security, economic and political involvements. It is in this context that the Indian State of Manipur has to be included. The place of Manipur within Indo-Myanmar connectivity represents a serious test for the Indian government—of its ability to impose its agenda, and of its sensitivity to local concerns. Stronger connectivity requires major infrastructure initiatives: *In one of India's most corrupt states, can rails and roads be done right? Stronger connectivity also requires recognition of the development needs of Manipuris: To what extent will such issues feature on India's connectivity agenda?*[15] The Indian government, in policy design and implementation, does not have a sterling record on these questions. And its leverage is greater over some bodies than others. But only the central government has the combination of resources and responsibilities to coordinate between, and try to shape the behaviour of, the various players of Manipur's political economy—interest groups in the central government itself, state authorities, the security establishment, and local underground and civil society players. Success in these efforts would demand special persistence and focus from Modi and his team, and from those who follow them. But the benefits could be enormous: a more stable and prosperous Manipur, emerging overland trade corridors to ASEAN, and new diplomatic leverage in East and Southeast Asia for other priorities. This only will make the Act East Policy successful.

Notes

1. Since Indian Prime Minister Narendra Modi came to power in May, he has sought to project to foreign-policy watchers a renewed commitment to India's Look East Policy (LEP)—or, as Modi's administration has renamed it, the "Act East Policy." The LEP was put forward in 1991 to reorient Indian foreign policy towards East Asia and Southeast Asia. But half-hearted commitment to the policy has severely restricted

India's footprint in these regions, even as Chinese influence destabilises Indian hegemony in South Asia. Major deals with Bangladesh and Japan, in addition to a flurry of meetings between top Indian officials and their regional counterparts, have been taken as early signs that Act East represents a genuine shift in Indian foreign policy. With Myanmar, deliverables under Modi thus far have been fairly modest: an agreement to crack down on regional insurgencies, a route-mapping exercise for the long-awaited Imphal-Mandalay bus service, and continued progress on the India-Myanmar-Thailand Trilateral Highway and Kaladan Multi-Modal Transit Project. The LEP framed Myanmar as India's overland bridge to the dynamic ASEAN belt, and Modi's rhetoric on Myanmar has stressed his dedication to realising this vision.

2. For details refer to http://www.mea.gov.in/Portal/ForeignRelation/Myanmar_May-2014.pdf (downloaded on January 16, 2015 at 10.00 pm).
3. For details see Gazette Notification No. G.S.R 611(E) of Ministry of Home Affairs dated July 21, 2010.
4. "Border Trade between India and Myanmar through Moreh: Its Trends and Problems," *Manipur Online*, Posted by Editor on Sunday, October 17, 2010 at 12:06 am.
5. "Indian and Myanmar delegates for Survey Work of Imphal-Mandalay bus service arrive in State," *Imphal Free Press*, January 12, 2015.
6. Directorate General of Foreign Trade (DGFT), Ministry of Commerce, Government of India has clarified (vide Policy Circular No. 53 (RE-99)/1997-2002 dated 29.02.2000 [PDF](5.5 kb)) that in addition to the provisions contained in the DGFT Public Notices Notification No. 9/95-Customs dated 6.3.1995 [PDF](12.21 kb) (for 22 items for border trade on Indo-Myanmar border) and Notification No. 62/2010-Customs dated 12.5.2010 [PDF](54.35 kb) (for additional 18 items). For details also refer to: OM No.570/04/2003 -LC dated 18.10.2010 of Shri M. Satish Kumar Reddy, Director (ICD), Central Board of Excise & Customs, Department of Revenue on "Conversion of border trade into normal trade at Indo-Myanmar Border Trade Points." The circular says: "The undersigned is directed to refer to Department of Commerce OM No.9/3/2009-FT (EA) dated 28.9.2010 on the above subject and to state that Moreh and Zokhawthar Land Customs Stations have been notified under Section 7 of the Customs Act, 1962 without any restriction regarding the mode of trade. Notification 9/95 Customs as amended by Notification 62/2010 Customs allows a concessional rate of duty of 5% ad valorem only on 40 items specified in the notification. However, normal trade can take place through the above LCSs as per the prevailing Foreign Trade Policy provisions and on payment of duty at applicable rates."
7. Zarini Mann, "Burma-Indo Border Market Threatened by Indian Insurgents," *The Irrawaddy*, Friday, July 5, 2013.
8. Edmund Downie, "Manipur and India's 'Act East' Policy," *The Diplomat*, February 25, 2015.
9. This border town had a population of 9,673 in 1991. It increased to 16,737 in 2001.
10. S. P. Shukla, "Transforming the Northeast—High Level Commission Report to the Prime Minister," New Delhi, 1997, pp. 83-84.
11. Akshat Kaushal, "Moreh: The gateway to Southeast Asia," *Business Standard*, February, 15, 2015.
12. Ibid.
13. Lee Lavina, "Myanmar's Transition to Democracy: New Opportunities or Obstacles for India?" *Contemporary Southeast Asia*, 2 (2014):290. eLibrary. Web. July 13, 2015.

14. Daniel Wagner et al., *Can China and India Coexist in Myanmar?* http://www.internationalpolicydigest.org/2014/02/20/can-china-india-coexist-myanmar/ (Retrieved on July 15, 2015).
15. Edmund Downie, op. cit., n. 8.

4

TOURISM AND NORTHEAST INDIA: ENHANCING CONNECTIVITY AND REGIONAL INTEGRATION PROCESS

Introduction

Tourism, today, is one of the most significant sectors where states can enhance cooperation and regional integration process. A general agreement has emerged that tourism not only increases foreign exchange income, but also creates employment opportunities and increases people-to-people contact. Due to the income and employment generating capacity it creates, tourism has got special significance for emerging economies and regions. This sector could play an important role in regional cooperation and integration of any region, without exception, of Northeast India (NEI) and Myanmar, the biggest country in mainland Southeast Asia—which had many things in common.[1] In his recent tour of Northeast India, Prime Minister Narendra Modi recognised the untapped tourism potential of the region, which could be transformed into a productive component of the region's economy. During the 29th Statehood Day of Arunachal Pradesh at Indira Gandhi Park, Itanagar on February 20, 2015 Prime Minister Modi said that the Centre was in the process of planning to turn Northeast India into an organic hub to boost agriculture production and to improve 2G, 3G and 4G connectivity in the region, which had been neglected for long.

Prime Minister Modi said that the Centre was proactive about Northeast and would initiate measures to bring the region's development on par with other developed parts of the country. He informed that the Centre was planning to convert the Northeast into an "Organic Hub" of the country to boost agriculture and horticulture production, keeping in view its conducive agro-climatic conditions, and had proposed the establishment of six new agricultural universities in the region. He said that the Government was planning to launch 18 new FM channels for the region for which an auction would be conducted soon. Besides, proposals had been made to improve 2G, 3G and 4G connectivity in the region.[2] The Prime Minister further announced that the Central government would provide Rs. 28,000 crores for laying down new railway lines strictly for improving connectivity, while the primary objective remained in developing the untapped tourism potential.[3] This act brings to the fore the significance of Northeast India as an important tourism hub which, if properly synchronised with the recent moves of its immediate neighbour, Myanmar, could be a tool for economic development of the whole region and, at the same time, an important contribution to India's Look East policy. In his quest to transform LEP into a more vibrant policy, Prime Minister Modi would take into consideration the tourism prospect of NEI as a growth engine. In his newly coined connotation of *Act East*, the tourism sector has got a significant place of its own. Tourism will undoubtedly bring peace, development and connectivity to the region. Thus, it is clear that Tourism remains one of the most important agendas of India's Look East Policy which is attracting political and economic attention. At the same time, with the development of Tourism in the Northeastern Region, India's neighbourhood policy, particularly with the Southeast Asian states, has to be enhanced, and here Myanmar again happens to be one of the major factors to link the tourism sector of India's Northeast with that of greater Southeast Asia.

An important objective of LEP in this era of globalisation and regional shifts is to develop greater economic cooperation with its Southeast Asian neighbours through people-to-people contact. In this context, tourism is an instrument of reciprocal growth, with the relevance of Northeast India and Myanmar in particular, and Southeast Asia in general, becoming pre-eminent. At the same time, more and more emphasis on the question of connectivity in the ever-improving India-ASEAN cooperation could be a strong stimulus. In spite of several problems, as discussed in the earlier chapters, there is a positive change in the political climate of Myanmar, with increasing receptiveness to the international community. At the same time, improving law and order in NEI provides a brighter prospect for movement of people in these adjoining regions. This could be a good sign for enhancement of cooperation between the two through tourism which, in turn, could bolster the overall economy of the entire area. So the argument that regionalism-tourism development linkage has mutual and causal relationships, which reinforce each other and assist in movement along the same trajectory, proved to be apt in this setting.[4] The incentives and benefits generated from the tourism industry encourage other sectors to develop, which generates a chain of spillover effects. It also connects regions through three dimensions: people, institutions and infrastructure.

Rationale

With the aforementioned background, a new prospect that one could see is the increasing importance of NEI where Myanmar retains a top precedence. The two share a boundary of 1,643 km. Any initiative taken under India's LEP could not weaken the importance of Myanmar's geostrategic position as India's land corridor to Southeast Asia, with India's Northeast as linkage. The same applies in the expectation of developing the tourism sector under this insurance. And, in the context of rising trend of regionalisation and liberalisation in South and Southeast Asia, NEI and Myanmar are all the more important for close and reciprocal cooperation in the promotion of tourism. Tourism is flourishing in the entire Southeast Asia, including in

Myanmar, and NEI could be a constituent of the milieu and garner the benefits. At the same time, NEI is home to a large-scale unexplored and untapped historical, cultural as well as natural assets which could be of high interest to tourists from Myanmar and beyond. Also in that location is the ethnic, racial and cultural affinity between the two. The unique but untapped natural endowments and colourful traditions of NEI, when combined with the vast cultural heritage of Myanmar, could provide a potential ground for boosting up the tourism sector both ways, which in turn would be a boon for bilateral economic cooperation and subsequent growth of both. The Northeast of India, besides being richly endowed with natural resources, is identified as one of the world's biodiversity hotspots, as it hosts species-rich tropical rainforests and supports diverse plant and fauna and several crop species.

Paired off with this is the diverse mix of cultural and tribal customs and civilisation. The increasing importance of NEI under India's LEP, and the gradual return to political stability and transition towards openness since 2010 in Myanmar, provides a positive ground for exploring and developing the tourism sector as a medium for further people-to-people contact, and, at the same time, for bilateral economic cooperation. As the cultural connections between the Northeastern states of India and the countries that stand to its East pre-existed the formation of nations in South Asia and continues to remain an important informal medium of link, this natural connection could be of advantage in furthering any relations between the two. Many of the tribes and sub-tribes of NEI residing in the border areas or inside are culturally and ethnically linked with those in Myanmar, and one could see lots of similarities in their ways of life. To take an example, one could see many from Nagaland state of India attending the Naga Festival held in January every year in the Naga-inhabited areas of Myanmar. Besides, NEI being a natural bridge between India and Southeast Asia, economic integration with its transnational neighbours (especially

Myanmar) is expected to open up new opportunities for the region, not excluding the tourism sector. At the same time, the initiative on the part of a politically stable Myanmar for adopting tourism as a priority area in its *Framework for Economic and Social Reforms* and *National Comprehensive Development Plan* could be a positive and reciprocal indication.[5] Thus, the very rationale of studying the future prospects for a collective tourism promotion of NEI and Myanmar is not only an interesting but obvious area. Thus, tourism can undoubtedly remain a vital growth engine to connect Northeast India with the rest of India in general, and the entire Southeast Asia and the Asia-Pacific region, in particular.

Tourism as a Growth Engine

That tourism is not only a growth engine but also an export growth engine and employment generator is a viewpoint accepted by the Governments of India and Myanmar in their joint quest for sustainable economic growth and upliftment of those lagging behind in society. According to the Economic Survey 2013-14, Government of India, as presented in Parliament, the tourism sector has capacity to create large-scale employment, both direct and indirect, for diverse sections in society, from the most specialised to the unskilled workforce. The sector contributed around 6.6 per cent of India's GDP in 2012 and supported 39.5 million jobs, which is 7.7 per cent of its total employment.[6] As positive news for the tourism sector in the northeastern states of the country, foreign tourist visits in the region grew by 27.9 per cent in 2013 over the previous year. The number of foreign tourist visits (FTVs) stood at 84,820 in 2013, as compared to 66,302 in 2012. The states had seen 12.5 per cent growth in 2012 over 2011, when the number stood at 58,920. Sikkim saw maximum FTVs at 31,698, followed by Assam (17,738), Tripura (11,853), Arunachal Pradesh (10,846) and Meghalaya (6,773). Among the eight northeastern states, the highest growth in FTVs during 2013 over 2012 was observed in

Manipur (154.7 per cent) followed by Arunachal Pradesh (111.2 per cent), Tripura (51.2 per cent), Nagaland (32.7 per cent), Meghalaya (27.5 per cent), Sikkim (19.7 per cent), Mizoram (7.5 per cent) and Assam (0.5 per cent).[7]

Northeast as a Unique Entity: What Can It Give?

The Northeast of India, which stretches from the foothills of the Himalayas in the Eastern range and is surrounded by Bangladesh, Bhutan, China, Nepal and Myanmar, comprises eight states, namely, Arunachal Pradesh, Assam, Manipur, Meghalaya, Mizoram, Nagaland, Tripura and Sikkim. Racially, inhabitants of the neighbourhoods are closer to its Eastern neighbours rather than to those in other regions of the Indian mainland. NEI has 3.1 per cent of India's total population and 8 per cent of the country's land area and is connected to the mainland by the Siliguri Corridor in West Bengal, with a width of only 21 to 40 km. Interestingly, however, the region has a long international boundary, about 96 per cent, with China and Bhutan in the North, Myanmar in the East, Nepal in the West and Bangladesh in the South and West. Thus with the right policy NEI could provide room for tourist visits from across the international line. This region can be considered as a melting pot of various ethnic cultures of different backgrounds, shaping the cultural heritage of the present inhabitants. The assimilation of cultures in the form of both material and non-material culture can be seen in every aspect of society and life. Early movements of people through this region might have contributed tremendously for this assimilation. Scholars like Medhi refer to this region as the "Great Indian Corridor," for the prehistoric and proto-historic movements of people from and to its neighbouring regions.[8] Not only this, NEI is also characterised by cultural and ethnic diversity of its own, which makes it more colourful and contributes a uniqueness of its own. The age-old practices and traditions that emerged from mixing institutionalised religions with the existing animism provide a distinct variety for outside people. Though proper balancing of tradition and modernity could be seen in various aspects of life in the region, yet there are still many untouched and virgin natural hotpots too, which would be a new variety for visitors. It is also important to understand here that while discussing Northeast India, one has to be careful about the sensitivity that persists there. The mainstream ideas may or may not be linked with the prevailing ideas that exist in the Northeastern region of India. Thus, the mainstream ideas must not be aggressive enough to grasp the Northeastern region in any form. The only thing the mainstream ideas can do is to link Northeastern ideas with themselves, and adopt them the way they are. Otherwise, problems may occur in linking the Northeastern region with mainstream Indian ideas and foreign policy. Mere implementation of armed forces in the Northeastern region and allocation of funds will not solve the problem. It is important for the government to link the common people and the stakeholders in the process of development of the Northeastern region, if there is at all a will on the part of Government of India to implement its Look East policy successfully. It is always important to remember that being a latecomer in the Indian mainstream, the region has remained less accessible to the outside world, which in itself is a boon in disguise in the present millennium. For a long time, it has been lucky enough to maintain most of its natural diversity. In fact, for the new and growing breed of tourists in the emerging globalised world, who are money-rich and time-poor, and seek a unique experience, the Northeast with its variety and uniqueness holds immense attraction. The rich natural beauty and its diversity, exotic cultural and ethnic mosaic, flora and fauna, and the serenity of the virgin and unexplored ecosystems provide possibilities of a totally different experience for tourists. And, of late, the significance of NEI as a unique and happening tourism hotspot has been recognised worldwide.

Initiatives for Connectivity and Linkage with Special Reference to Northeast India and Myanmar

The fact remains that for development of tourism as a medium of cooperation and shared prosperity between NEI and Southeast Asia, Myanmar will remain an efficient medium of connectivity. This is because what is important today is the establishment of overland connectivity. Indeed, overland connectivity is going to be the main instrument that could bring people, infrastructure and economies closer to each other, which in turn will be a boon for the tourism sector. Thus, as an outcome of its connection with the various regional groupings when NEI and Myanmar come under the purview of many infrastructure projects taken up under a wide range of programmes, it could pave the way for a regionalism-tourism nexus. As such the initiatives that have been taken up by Government of India as well as the Governments of the States under LEP, which is mainly concerned with the concept of the Northeast as the outlet, started first in the form of developing connectivity and linkage. Every stakeholder in these parts realises now the indispensability of infrastructure for connectivity which, in a way, could play a crucial role in developing the tourism industry. The same applies to Myanmar where initiatives are on for synchronising its grand designs associated with its tourism sector under its ambitious *Tourism Master Plan* with that of ASEAN's objective of transforming ASEAN region to an ASEAN Economic Community by 2015. In the process it also comes under the *Master Plan for ASEAN Connectivity*. However, in the ongoing initiatives for a smooth ASEAN-India connectivity, maximum missing link is in NEI and Myanmar. In India, the connectivity within the NEI is extremely poor. The quality of national highways is quite negligible in most of the NEI states, though initiatives and subsequent improvements could be seen. The Centre has envisaged connecting the NEI state capitals to the East-West Highway through the Seven Sisters Corridor project. This will link the capitals of the eight states and the border points of Bhutan, Bangladesh and Myanmar. To channelise it, an ambitious programme of road-building has been taken up under the *Special Accelerated Road*

Development Programme for the Northeast (SARDP-NE) which was further supplemented by Pradhan Mantri Gram Sadak Yojna (PMGSY). In the Third BIMSTEC Summit held in Nay Pyi Taw in March 2014, the then Indian Foreign Minister, Salman Khurshid, highlighted the need for providing connectivity for seamless movement between India's Northeast and Myanmar. Initiatives in this direction were actually taken up a decade before, and the demand now is for further improvement. In 2001, India constructed the 160 km-long Tamu-Kalewa-Kalemyo highway, named *Indo-Myanmar Friendship Road.* Plans for a 1,400 km-long Trans-Asian Highway (TAH) that will connect India, Myanmar and Thailand is now being finalised. Work is also going on for a railway link that will connect Jiribam to Moreh and beyond up to Hanoi, as a part of the Trans-Asian Railways Project (TAR). Bilateral cooperation between India and Myanmar has also been expanding at a significant rate since 2001. Some major projects between the two, besides the one already mentioned, include the Rhi-Tiddim and Rhi-Falam Roads in Myanmar and the *Kaladan Multimodal Transport Project.* The Kaladan Multimodal Transit-cum-Transport project agreement which was signed in April 2008 will help increase connectivity between the two countries. This project will link landlocked Northeast India to the sea through Myanmar. It also envisages the development of a 225-km waterway on the Kaladan River and the construction of ports along the way. During the conduct of this project two major visits have been made. One, visit to Moreh-Tamu Border, which has been discussed in the preceding chapter. The positive scene we have seen in the Moreh-Tamu Border is that Government of India will now allow free movement of Myanmarese citizens up to Moreh town in Manipur. At the same time Government of Myanmar will allow Indians to enter up to Tamu Town. The necessary amount has been sanctioned for expansion of the *Integrated Check Post* in Moreh. It is believed that the Imphal-Mandalay bus service will start this year though the proposal was accepted way back in 2006, and the exact date has been postponed. It also came to our notice that some private tour agencies[9] are now organising Imphal to Mandalay trips at a very cheap rate, with necessary sanctions from both the Government agencies. The second important survey that was conducted during this study was the visit to India-Myanmar border trading point at Rih-Zokhawthar in Mizoram.[10] The distance between Aizawl and Champhai is 192 km approximately, whereas the distance between Champhai and Zokhawthar is approximately 23 km through the Border Road. During the study, a visit was made from Aizawl to Champhai (23 km from the Indo-Myanmar Border) which took approximately nine hours to reach through hilly roads. When a visit was made to Zokhawthar, which is a border area, from Champhai, it took nearly two hours to cover 23 km. It is true that NEI has immense potential for tourism, but at the same time it is important to understand that local support is very much required to implement the true sense of tourism in NEI compared to the other regions of Southeast Asia, such as Kuala Lumpur or Bangkok. As indicated earlier, land contact is important to establish tourism as a source of income in the NER. But, at the same time, it has to be remembered that the porous border between India and Myanmar is a great security concern where most of the illegal trade is taking place. There is no such record in the Customs offices both at the Moreh and Zokhawthar borders. In Zokhawthar the legal border trade between both the countries is approximately US$ 20,000 per month, whereas the informal and illegal trade through these two borders is huge compared to the legal trade. Corruption is the first important factor which restricts growth in the NER. The Government in New Delhi has no idea how corruption is taking hold in the Northeastern Region. During our visit a question was asked of the District Commissioner of Champhai on the issue of corruption on the border, and he refused to respond.[11] Similarly, when the Superintendent of Police (SP) of Champhai District[12] was asked about the illegal trade and what kind of action had been taken by the government to restrict it, the reply was that since the border was highly porous, it was very difficult to control the illegal trade and the trafficking in arms and drugs. He further informed that during the last year, 3-4 cases had been filed and a few porters had been captured carrying AK-47 and M-Series arms. He said that many of these M-Series were made in Cambodia, and he was not very sure whether these arms are coming from China or not. From the comments made by the Superintendent of Police at Champhai District, the possibility that China had established an arms factory at Cambodia could not be ignored at this stage. The Superintendent of Police further informed that a public announcement system existed in the entire Border district, and sometimes the NGOs played an important role in identifying illegal migrants in the Border region to help identify the illegal traders. It is evident that the porters who carry these illegal arms or drugs have no idea where it is actually coming from. The Major of Assam Rifles at Champhai is of the same view, since the Border was porous, illegal trafficking and trade cannot be controlled at this stage.[13] The trust between the two countries, India and Myanmar, has to be enhanced at the political level, and joint operations will eradicate the adverse forces that operate in the region to disturb India's political and security interests. Undoubtedly, this will also help Myanmar to enhance its national security, and Myanmar has a positive role to play in this regard. Myanmar cannot just satisfy both India and China at the same time. It is important for Myanmar to help India because culturally and politically the structures of India and Myanmar are more or less the same. When Myanmar is progressing towards democracy, it is important for Myanmar to strengthen the hands of democratic forces to establish peace in the region. The recent trend of increasing cooperation between India and Myanmar directly across the border points along the boundary of Northeast India could be a means for easy accessibility in each other's areas. In addition, exploring and developing new points—Lungwa/Ledo, Pongru and Pokhungri in Nagaland and Nampong, Vijayanagar and Khimiyang in Arunachal Pradesh—is needed. The Manipur Commerce and Industries Minister had proposed an alternative border point in Behiang in Manipur's Churachandpur district along the Indo-Myanmar border, which needs consideration.[14] All this could to a certain extent provide the necessary connectivity and infrastructure for promoting people-to-people contact across borders, and at the same time, become an avenue for boosting the different dimensions of tourism. Thus, it is no exaggeration to say that once all these factors materialise, tourism cooperation between India's Northeast and Myanmar will be greatly enhanced.

Picture 4.1: Road Condition of the Border Road from Champhai to Zokhawthar. (Photo taken on June 23, 2015)

The above environment, situations, initiatives and dynamics, gradually unfolding in the region, both with governmental and non-governmental initiatives, bound no longer within political boundaries, may bring about a prospective tourism scenario. Though India and Myanmar as such have no specific bilateral relations in the tourism sector, both countries are part and parcel of the tourism initiatives taken under the various regional and subregional groupings mentioned. As such there are lots of mutually beneficial areas, for Northeast India and Myanmar, in the tourism sector which could be developed to the optimum if subregional groups could provide the right framework and the much needed platform. This could be a positive driver to the existing question of a NEI-Myanmar tourism synergy. In the case of Myanmar, although it possesses diverse and extensive cultural, natural, and historic assets, it has only recently begun to develop its enormous tourism potential. As a result of sweeping political and economic reforms, the country is enjoying unprecedented tourism growth. It was in 2012 that, for the first time in its history, Myanmar received over 1 million international visitors. Earnings from international tourism more than quintupled from $165 million in 2008 to $1.1 billion in 2014, though it still has to go a long way.[15] By comparison, among the ASEAN countries, tourism's total contribution to the GDP is still the lowest in Myanmar, coming to only 3.7 per cent in 2013.[16] Need is felt for more key drivers of tourism growth which include the rapid expansion of scheduled inbound flights, eased tourist visa-on-arrival privileges at gateway airports, improving business and investment conditions, to grow the demand for international travel among regional and long-haul markets.[17] Further, Government of Myanmar is pondering the declaration of 2016 as *Visit Myanmar Year*, reviving what it did in 1996. In fact, today Myanmar is eager to pursue an enhanced regional cooperation in tourism and related sectors in order to exchange knowledge and lessons on good practices, ensure consistency in tourism standards and visa policies, and harmonise the collection and reporting of tourism statistics.

Picture 4.2: The Rhi-Zokhawthar Border. Photo taken on June 23, 2015

The same is the case with India, in general, and Northeast India, in particular. India started its National Tourism Policy in 2002 which was subsequently followed by the formation of National Tourism Advisory

Council (NTAC), which serves as a think tank of the Ministry of Tourism for the development of tourism in the country. Not only this, Government of India's executing agency for the Northeast, the Northeastern Council (NEC), has also taken up policies for enhancement of tourism for overall economic growth of the region under its *Vision 2020*. Ministry of Development for Northeast (DONER) strongly emphasised the *Comprehensive Tourism Master Plan 2011* initiated by NEC, to be implemented in three phases over a period of ten years. Besides, the present Modi government is in favour of promoting *Make in Northeast* initiative within the scope of his reoriented *Act East,* which could be a new dimension for the promotion of tourism in NEI.[18]

At the present juncture clear initiatives on the part of both the Governments of India and Myanmar could be seen for transforming tourism as a long-term growth engine in their respective countries. In the *Annual Report 2013-14* (Ministry of Tourism), it has been mentioned clearly that the effort of Tourism Policy of India is that of "positioning tourism as a major engine of economic growth and harnessing its direct and multiplier effects on employment and poverty eradication in a sustainable manner by active participation of all segments of the society... ."[19] At the same time, Myanmarese Government, in its *Tourism Master Plan 2013-2020,* clearly envisioned transforming tourism as a growth engine and using it to pull up the country's economy with available potential. To make its objectives more effective the Master Plan has been linked to the *ASEAN Tourism Strategic Plan* and, in particular, to the *ASEAN Tourism Marketing Strategy*. Experts do believe that this will promote Myanmar's tourism within a regional initiative which in turn could help in promoting the country's tourism development in the long run. Ultimately, in this emerging dynamics, because of where they are geostrategically tagged together, NEI and Myanmar are inseparable from each other in the matter of development in the region. The fact remains that there is indeed ample scope for both in using the tourism sector as a medium of growth through mutual cooperation. Thus, keeping all these in mind, every effort is needed from the side of the stakeholders for creating the right synergy between these two. Sorting out the shortcomings, while identifying the positive points, and boosting them up, will go a long way. Though NEI and Myanmar have many things in common, they are yet unique in their own way, and in this sense each has their specific areas to contribute. However, the China factor will play an important role in linking NER with Myanmar. Due to the long history of attachment, China will continue to have an overriding influence in Myanmar regardless of India's efforts to build a win-win relationship. In other words, as long as India and China have a peaceful and constructive relationship, India-Myanmar relations will flourish in the present political dispensation.[20] This is because historically China was involved in Myanmar through the Burma Communist Party (BCP). The BCP, however, was only a communist party in name and was actually projecting Chinese interests. The year 1989 changed the nature of the relationship, and China started to help with ceasefire agreements. The price was more autonomy to the border regions and their integration with Southern China's economy. As described by Egreteau, the advent of the new Junta in Yangon after the 1988 uprising and the 1989 Tiananmen massacre made the two nations seek mutual relations in the face of world isolation and criticism.[21] The relationship started with a trade agreement in order to open up the provinces of Yunnan and Sichuan that are linked with Myanmar through the Irrawaddy River as well as by road and rail links. There are large numbers of Chinese investors and traders throughout northern Myanmar, as well as an important Myanmar Chinese Diaspora. Chinese ambition is further evident in the Indian Ocean, helping Myanmar to modernise its naval bases at Hanggyi, the Cocos Islands, Akyab and Mergui. Today, it is unclear, however, as to how far the various ministries understand China's economic and strategic involvement in Myanmar.[22] The power vacuum in Kachin state which has allowed the economy in northern Myanmar to be integrated with Yunnan province is not generally understood in New Delhi. The Ministry of External Affairs seems to rely on the fact that the Myanmar government wants to balance out China's influence with relations across ASEAN and with India. This, however, is not enough as India has to be seen to be proactive in developing the ties, just as China has been. India needs to take advantage of this fact rather than let the opportunity slide by. Today, it is important to identify that Bangladesh and Myanmar have been the key transit routes through which small arms made in China reach the Northeast. The main conduits in Myanmar are the Karen National Union (KNU) and the Kachin Independence Army (KIA). These two ethnic insurgent groups have acted as the interlocking chain for the illegal weapons flow from Yunnan in China via Myanmar to Northeast India, but the most effective illegal weapons trader in Myanmar is another armed ethnic group, the United Wa State Army (UWSA). Bangladesh under the regime of the Awami League can be trusted by India, because historically Awami League has supported India in eliminating anti-Indian forces that operate on Bangladeshi soil. For, example, the base of ULFA chief Paresh Barua was eliminated and destroyed by the Bangladesh government under Awami League. But the question is, how to trust Myanmar? Can Myanmar enhance cooperation with India by negating the Chinese anti-Indian forces operating on Myanmarese land? These questions are critical and need answers at this stage.

However, India must slowly enhance cooperation with Myanmar because of its recent democratic pattern of government.

An Assessment

If the purpose of any foreign bilateral policy is to encourage a change of course for the other, India's engagement of Myanmar has met with moderate, but far from spectacular, success. In security terms, India can be assured that Myanmar has not become a "client state" of China, that formal links between the two countries' respective armed forces have grown, as well as be assured of cross-border cooperation on arms and drug trafficking. On the important issue of counter-insurgency cooperation, however, Myanmar gives all the right assurances but has somehow failed to deliver. As long as insurgents can find safe haven across the border, New Delhi's ambitions to bring peace and development to its Northeast will remain unfulfilled. While China has been able to effectively pressure Myanmar to control its eastern border regions, the spoils to be had from border trade with the Northeast—one of the most underdeveloped regions in India —simply have not compared to those from China's thriving Yunnan Province. Economically, India will be pleased with the steady increase in trade between the two countries, and with the expanding portfolio of investments it has been able to make in Myanmar's oil and gas sector. However, the major prize of securing direct access to gas reserves and hydropower for electricity generation for the Northeast has so far eluded New Delhi largely due to circumstances beyond its control. Unfortunately, the lack of progress on the many visionary connectivity projects initiated by India cannot be blamed on third parties. Myanmar has not given these projects high priority thus far, with only one—the 160-km Moreh-Kalewa Road into Chin State—having been completed in 2001.

Myanmar's transition to democracy and a liberalised economy seemingly opens up tantalising opportunities for trade, investment and energy security for India. The scale of Myanmar's development needs will mean that India's ambitious Sittwe Port, Kaladan multimodal highway, and trilateral highway projects are likely to be well supported by a prospective National League for Democracy (NLD) government. Increased border trade and infrastructure building to connect Myanmar's economy to both India and ASEAN can only be viewed as positive developments for the country's people. Just as the junta was keen to improve relations with India to maintain a level of foreign policy autonomy from China, the same can also be expected of the NLD.

Indian companies also have an opportunity to capitalise on community concerns about Chinese investment by demonstrating a greater level of social responsibility and desire to ensure greater community benefit in the implementation of resource projects.

Many obstacles, however, still remain to be overcome before an optimistic assessment about the prospects for India-Myanmar relations can be given, even if the NLD takes power in 2015. Myanmar is likely to continue to be a safe haven for Indian insurgents, given that Myanmar has its own interests in allowing them to operate in the borderlands. Moreover, the NLD does not appear to have a credible plan to come to a political settlement with ethnic insurgent groups, and until a permanent peace is brought to the borderlands, insurgents will continue to operate there. Economically, while the NLD has shown that it is committed to greater liberalisation, and expanding opportunities for trade and foreign investment, even where projects are unpopular, there is still a long way to go to create the conditions for substantial growth in relations between the two countries. It will take some time to improve the rule of law and tackle endemic corruption. Efforts must still be made to break the monopolies of military conglomerates and "cronies," expose state-owned enterprises to competition, and create open processes for the awarding of resource licences, all of which, if done too confrontationally, or too quickly, may trigger yet another military coup.[23]

However, today, the ever-increasing involvement of tourism in socio-economic development, and the political willingness to raise such an industry, encourage other sectors to grow. It is proceeding from national to regional level in terms of planning, management and growth. That is where Myanmar and NEI have to fit. Tourism related activities make up a significant part of regional cooperation and consolidation process. Such regional tourism development becomes part of overall regional growth in which the public and private sectors work together to ease the movement of tourists, goods and services. Taking into consideration the existing wave of regionalism there could be a combination of the tourism prospects—the already existing ones as well as those that can emerge—of the two regions of mutual interest, to give it the shape of a mutual goal. Going along with this line of thinking one could come to the hypothesis that tourism could be a powerful growth engine for both NEI and Myanmar, specifically, and the benefit will be immense and greater if the two meaningfully cooperate with each other and deliver a regional framework in the context of tourism promotion. As for Myanmar, tourism development has been set inside a broad national framework which prioritises, both in the micro as well as macro level, purposeful growth of quality tourism through strategic and responsible actions to deliver equitable economic benefits, social welfare, and environmental sustainability. It is for India within its LEP to streamline tourism in the Northeast to these new moves of Myanmar. What is asked for the country is an effective tourism controlling body run in the demarcation of public-private-partnership (PPP) model with strict emphasis on accountability, sustainability, income generation and ultimately economic growth. Government of India and the state governments in the Northeast should initiate the right mechanism and air so that the private actors could come alive in exploring and extending job opportunities in this sector with more emphasis to PPP models of evolution. For all this, connectivity needs to be improved, which again depends on the proper implementation of projects within a time frame. Above all, rules and ordinances should be such that more people are allowed to travel to the regions but without compromising the area-specific unique culture and inheritance of the locals. Aside from all these, despite the fact that, for many years, NEI and Myanmar had been beset by problems relating to law and order and lack of development, both the regions are home to a large youthful population forming a major lump of the region's human resources. With the correct type of skill development initiatives and capacity development mechanism, the available human resources could be transformed into productive forces without the exclusion of the tourism sector, therefore leading to the development of their respective economic systems. Finally, tourism needs to be raised in such a fashion that it contributes to the overall development of the area. And this could aptly support the viewpoint in Vision 2020, that is, to return NEI to the status of the national economic eminence that it held till a few decades ago; to fashion the development process then that growth springs from and spreads out to the grassroots; and to ascertain that the region acts as the arrowhead role, it must work in the new wave of the country's Look East policy. Since the central elements of tourism development are the state, market, tourists, infrastructure and local peoples, there requires to be a proper synchronisation of all these factors. Both Track I and Track II initiatives are a must. At this juncture what is needed is that stakeholders on both sides work for a coherence of policies and initiatives linked with tourism cooperation and development of the two regions collectively, and at the same time negativities are sensitised to the utmost. Racial, ethnic, cultural and historical affinity between those in NEI and Myanmar could be used as positive drivers through the medium of tourism for reducing poverty and bringing shared prosperity in the intact area. Although different states have different attitudes and policies towards tourism development, yet the common fact is that tourism needs to be wielded in an effective, responsible, people-centric and sustainable manner. But then the whole exercise leading towards pragmatic and effective tourism cooperation between India's Northeast and Myanmar could be effective, creating more views for the future within the close up of India's LEP, in general, and Myanmar policy, in particular. This requires a strong political will and more people-to-people contact. India's Northeast is the country's only region to share a land border with Myanmar, and it is therefore not unexpected that ground realities in the Northeast would influence Indian policy towards Myanmar. That this 1,643-km border is porous, largely hilly and jungle-infested, used by separatist ethnic insurgents and those who smuggle narcotics drugs and weapons in large quantities, makes it all the more important that India would expect Myanmar to address these issues pertaining to India's security, especially in the country's Northeast. The flow of weapons and drugs from Myanmar to India through the borders of its northeastern states has prompted New Delhi to push the Tatmadaw-led military regime in Myanmar to block trafficking of this dangerous contraband in the past. India has also periodically raised the issue of its northeastern ethnic insurgents using bases in Myanmar's Sagaing division and other states and called for firm action, just as Bhutan and Bangladesh have taken against Indian insurgents in recent years.

Now, today, there are certain issues upon which we need to concentrate, involving India's northeastern region when it comes to the country's relations with Myanmar. It is important to advocate the following issues: (a) more trans-border trade across land customs points through Northeast India and neighbouring Myanmar provinces to help create a "bona fide economy" on the borders, (b) greater and effective security cooperation between India and Myanmar as well as between provincial governments running border states and divisions on the borders of the two countries, (c) a joint effort to tackle the problems of weapons and drugs on this 1,600 km border, (d) to facilitate a relaxed trans-border regime for movement of tribal communities with kinsmen across the borders, (e) to situate the border regions in the proposed BCIM economic corridor to facilitate speedy growth. Myanmar and India share deep cultural, religious and historical bonds. Without being overtly drawn into a messy competition with the Chinese, India needs to play its cards well, as Myanmar is vital to India's wider economic and geostrategic interests.

At the same time, it is important for us to realise that the rapid change in the nature of tourists, the tourism industry and its interrelation with the instinctive and cultural environment necessitates new paradigms to manage tourism development. Development of tourism—especially during the final quarter of the twentieth century—has also rightly evoked concerns about sociocultural and environmental impacts of tourism at macro and micro levels. Could there be a path to build up bonds between different target groups such as tourists, tourism developers, tourism service providers and host community?

The spirit behind such development should be humanising. Scholars have argued that sustainable tourism requires a spectrum of experiences, supply characteristics, and market requirements. Fuller understanding of the functional markets and of the consumer has important research and market implications and is vital to the evolution of suitable services. Appropriate services lead to more value-added products and higher positive economic impact. In other words the concept of sustainable tourism embodies a challenge to get the world's tourism capacity and character of its products without adversely affecting the environment that sustains and nurtures them. The very idea speaks that the needs of today's visitors should not be played at the expense of future generations. In full, sustainable tourism development (STD) advocates proper exploitation and an explanation of touristic resources and the management of development should be as per the need, not only of the present, but also of the future. For the formulation of a sustainable tourism strategy in the Northeast region, tourism planners may need to concentrate on some key areas like: (a) conservation and neo-interpretation of natural, archaeological/historical and cultural tourism products, (b) seasonality aspects of tourism operation, (c) enhancement of tourist facilities and services (transportation, accommodation, etc.), (d) public health and safety, (e) promotion of tourism infrastructure,(f) focus on community involvement, (g) allocating/zoning spaces for recreational land use,(h) extending efforts on need-based tourism education and training, (i) tourism financing, (j) prioritisation of domestic tourism sector, and (k) evolving strategies for better management of the sector.

Despite having a comparatively long history of tourism, most of the tourism authorities in Northeast India have not gained much experience in planning, developing and managing the tourism sector. Consequently, in most cases, their efforts in tourism promotion are misdirected and waste the valuable resources of the region. Amidst political quarters, local tourism promoters and managers in some parts of the region, the image of tourism development is attraction-centric rather than based on a sound and organised developmental perspective. As a result, the region is not in a position to offer a better experience to tourists. Successful development and operation of the tourism sector in this region requires better management at the local government level to guide, facilitate and coordinate the process, so that tourism ventures can sustain in local socio-economic situation and contribute meaningfully in the areas concerned. Creation of a band of promoters and policymakers is also the need of the hour. It can be done by extending need-based tourism education and short and long-term tourism manpower development strategies which will help in producing an organised tourism sector in the region capable of giving the fruit of tourism to the tourists as also the locals. Hence, adoption of a sustainable tourism strategy is an urgent need to utilise the tourism potential of the northeastern region of India.[24] With the increasing intensity of the emergency in the Northeast, there is a pressing need to devise long-term, sustainable solutions for the region. A large part of the emergence arises from economic need, and hence the solution lies in economic (and social) development of the region. However, for economic development to take place, several key players need to step up and take the initiative.

The government will have to facilitate an ecosystem based industry where business practices can pass smoothly and without hassle, if there is really a will to make grow the concept of tourism in the Northeast. Despite various efforts by the Governments at the Central and at the State levels to enhance local development, the current strategy has guided to a distribution-oriented, politically-led economic process and not the efficiency-led process envisioned. This has resulted in natural resources and savings moving away from the region to other high productivity areas. Dependence on the Central Government for finances and work has passed into a passive attitude towards development in the States. The burden should be transferred to the local government agencies to create a sense of responsibility and ownership over economic activities to make growth. Also, commercial enterprises and social entrepreneurs should use the jumper cable in starting enterprises which affect the local community. For the self-sustained growth of a region, a thriving entrepreneurial ecosystem is required which is capable of forming business strategies, to contextualise them for local needs, and to create systems of demand and supply for the area. There also needs to be the existence of a market—where entrepreneurs can target their goods and services and consumers can get the things that they ask. By concentrating on economic factors (but not ignoring political and cultural elements) like labour cost, comparative advantages, technology, and efficiency, such a market can be grown within the Northeast.

While the hidden talents stored in the Northeast have recently been highlighted through a range of platforms, set up mostly by civil society actors, the market in the Northeast comes with its challenges. Cheap Chinese imports have flooded the marketplace, causing a drop in demand for local wares, and local artisans are slowly losing ground. To allow local entrepreneurs to get to such emerging markets, there needs to be a significant thrust towards the growth of a relationship between the rest of the State and people from this area. Such a long-term relationship will not only go to the founding of a true marketplace for local craftsmen and entrepreneurs, but will also assist in creating employment opportunities and the growth of the tourism sector in the area.[25]

Note: Some of the ideas of this chapter have been developed by Dr. Langpoklakpam Suraj Singh, Assistant Professor, Department of Political Science, D. M. College of Arts, Imphal, Manipur, who is associated with this project in various capacities including the field visits. Dr. Singh shared some of his ideas in the Conference held at Indian Institute of Technology, Guwahati (IITG) organised by the Jadavpur Association of International Relations (JAIR), supported by External Publicity Division, Ministry of External Affairs, Government of India, Maulana Abul Kalam Azad Institute of Asian Studies (MAKAIAS), Kolkata, Indian Council of Social Science Research (ICSSR), New Delhi and Indian Council of World Affairs (ICWA), New Delhi.

Notes

1. Langpoklakpam Suraj Singh, "Prospects of Northeast India-Myanmar Tourism Co-operation in the Emerging Dynamics of India's Look East Policy: A New Dimension," *JAIR Journal of International Relations*, issue 2, vol. 1, January 2015-June 2015.
2. "Prime Minister Narendra Modi promises to develop Northeast into organic hub," *The Times of India*, 2015.
3. *The Sangai Express* (Imphal), December 2, 2014.
4. L. Suraj Singh, n. 1.
5. Ministry of Hotels and Tourism, Myanmar, "Myanmar: Tourism Master Plan 2013-2020" (Nay Pyi Taw: 2013), p. 3.
6. http://zeenews.india.com/business/indian-budget-2014/economic-survey-2013-14-stable-govt-global-economic-recovery-can-help-indian-tourism_103523.html. (Accessed on December 2, 2014.)
7. Yuthika Bhargava, "Northeast India sees spike in foreign tourist visits," *The Hindu*, August 5, 2014.
8. D. K. Medhi, "Potters and pottery of the Assam region," in J. Miksic (ed.), *Earthenware of Southeast Asia* (Singapore: NUS Press, 2003), pp. 322-35. 106
9. For example, refer this Facebook page retrieved on July 27, 201, https://www.facebook.com/www.kbenterprise.co.in
10. Field trip was organised on June 21, 2015-June 25 2015 by the Jadavpur Association of International Relations and Maulana Abul Kalam Azad Institute of Asian Studies (MAKAIAS), Kolkata.
11. Meeting with the District Commissioner on June 23, 2015 at Champhai Circuit House by Dr. Imankalyan Lahiri and his team.
12. Meeting with the Superintendent of Police on June 23, 2015 at Champhai Circuit House by Dr. Imankalyan Lahiri and his team.
13. Meeting with the Major of Assam Rifles at Champhai District on June 23, 2015 at Circuit House, Champhai, Mizoram.
14. "Linking India's Northeast with Southeast Asia: Significance of Internal Connectivity & Backward Integration," Issue Brief, IPCS, http://www.ipcs.org/issue-brief/southeast-asia/linking-indias-northeast-with-southeast-asia-significance-of-internal-connectivity-175.html. (Accessed on September 20, 2014.)
15. "ADB Releases: A Report on Myanmar Sustainable Tourism Development," Mekong Tourism, http://www.mekongtourism.org/news/myanmar/adb-releases-report-myanmar-sustainable-tourism-development. Also see, http://asiancorrespondent.com/129704/flights-

e-visas-drive-massive-growth-of-tourism-in-burma/. (Accessed on February 18, 2015.)

16. "World Travel and Tourism Council, Travel and Tourism Economic Impact 2014—Myanmar" (London: 2014), p. 8.
17. Ministry of Hotels and Tourism, Myanmar, "Myanmar: Tourism Master Plan 2013-2020" (Nay Pyi Taw: 2013).
18. L. Suraj, Singh, n. 1.
19. Ministry of Tourism, Government of India, Annual Report 2013-14 (New Delhi), p. 4.
20. Presentation made by Col. R. Hariharan (retd.) at an interaction on "Emerging India-China-Myanmar Relations," jointly organised by the Chennai Centre for China Studies (www.c3sindia.org) and the Department of International Relations of Stella Maris College, Chennai, at the college on July 19, 2007.
21. B. R., Nanda (ed.), *Indian Foreign Policy—the Nehru Years* (New Delhi: Vikas Publishing House, 1976), p. 16.
22. Marie Lall, "India-Myanmar Relations—Geopolitics and Energy in Light of the New Balance of Power in Asia," ISAS Working Paper, No. 29, January 2, 2008.
23 L. Lavina, "Myanmar's Transition to Democracy: New Opportunities or Obstacles for India?" *Contemporary Southeast Asia* (2), 290, August 1, 2014. Retrieved from http://elibrary.bigchalk.com
24. Prasanta Bhattacharya, "Tourism Development in Northeast India: Changing Recreational Demand, Developmental Challenges and Issues Associated with Sustainability." Available at: http://himalaya.socanth.cam.ac.uk/collections/journals/ebhr/pdf/EBHR_32_07.pdf (Retrieved on June 15, 2015).
25. "The Changing Face of North East India." Available at http://india.ashoka.org/changing-face-north-east-india (Retrieved on June 17, 2015). Photo: Dr. Imankalyan Lahiri

5
CONCLUSION

The previous chapter of this present research work has proved that the Look East Policy (LEP) was not driven by the needs of India's Northeast. It was a national policy necessitated by post-Cold War recalculations that found the country in a disadvantageous position vis-à-vis the fast developing countries of Southeast Asia. It was also partly driven by the need to counter overarching Chinese influence in the region. Thus it started as a foreign policy initiative of the government of India based on the idea of greater economic engagement and integration with countries of South Asia and Southeast Asia. The policy by its implications involves engineering economic programming, socio-political changes and a role for Northeast India as the overland gateway to South and Southeast Asia. But the fact that the LEP has made no significant impact on economic growth and peace in the Northeast is a matter that needs critical examination. It has to be scrutinised in light of the government's obligations and the problems and challenges that have been a feature of its engagement with the region. Central to this issue is the question of peace in Northeast India—positive peace that would be a contributory factor for the fruitful involvement of the region in the LEP. It seems to have been assumed that a greater economic participation resulting from the LEP would, automatically, remove much of the problems in Northeast India. But that such an assumption can only result in the policy becoming a non-starter has been proven by the lethargic economic impact on the Northeast. The security-related issues ensuing from unresolved, protracted conflicts may become an alibi for bypassing the region. Even as the country projects itself to the neighbouring Southeast Asian nations, apparently, there is no expressed strategy in the LEP seeking to resolve the conflicts in the Northeast systematically. This lack of a methodical approach to peace and conflict resolution relegates to the periphery the involvement and engagement of the region in the LEP.[1]

The preceding chapters clearly prove that the post-Cold War world order entailed new forms of relations amongst nations and regional groupings. In other words, regional integration became an essential feature of many of the regions of the world to survive geopolitically in the changed state of international affairs. After India opened up her market to the global liberal economy in 1991, realising the importance of the ASEAN market and also the need to counter the growing Chinese influence, it began to foster deeper relations with the Southeast Asian nations. The policy was already in motion the then Prime Minister Narasimha Rao made a series of visits to China, Japan, South Korea, Vietnam and Singapore. The policy received added impetus with India becoming a Sectoral Dialogue Partner with the Association of South East Asian Nations (ASEAN) in 1992 on trade, investment, tourism, science and engineering. In 2003 while giving a speech at the Harvard University the then former Foreign Minister, Yaswant Singh, with regard to LEP said: "In the past, India's engagement with much of Asia, including Southeast and East Asia, was built on an idealistic conception of Asian brotherhood, based on shared experiences of colonialism and of cultural ties. The rhythm of the region today is determined, however, as much by trade, investment and production as by history and culture. That is what motivates our decade-old 'Look East Policy.'"[2] It was the high-level meeting on the Look East Policy convened on October 31, 2007, under the Chairmanship of Pranab Mukherjee, the then Minister for External Affairs, with the presence of Ministers for DONER (Development of North Eastern Region), Chief Ministers of all Northeast states and the concerned Union Ministers, which was the first comprehensive consideration of the policy. Pranab Mukherjee, in his opening statement stated that, "the government is looking at a new paradigm of development where our foreign policy initiatives blend seamlessly into our national economic development."[3] Underpinning these concerns was a consensus that the Northeastern states should first try to develop its connectivity with each other and to develop its infrastructure at all levels.[4] As a result, the North Eastern Region Vision 2020 came about. Manmohan Singh, the then India's Prime Minister, remarked that, "This century is going to be Asia's century and that China and India are going to be major economies of this century. This is borne out by any number of studies and forecasts. This is part of our 'Look-East' policy."[5]

All the contemporary studies on Northeast India consider the Look East Policy as important; this is evident from the literature and available data. It has assumed critical importance to comprehend the policy in order to evolve an understanding of its impact on the people and their lives. The statist argument that fostering deeper economic and cultural and historical affiliations with the Southeast Asian nations will not only promote better economic opportunities for the area but also assist in containing separatist movements is belied by ground realities. The state of political, socio-economic conditions—six decades old unresolved problems of insurgency, mis-governance, corruption, unaccountability, militarisation and culture of impunity, lack of infrastructure in basic public delivery systems, including absence of reliable transport and communication facilities—inform the living conditions in the area. The field trip conducted during this study clearly proved that in the absence of an accountable socio-economic policy and adequate mechanisms for the welfare of the people in the region, chances are high that they may face more survival threats because of the continued conflict between the Central government, State governments and the non-state players. The survey conducted during this study also contends that unless the masses bear an equal part of the developmental space in the existing state structure, the promise of economic evolution through a regional arrangement with the neighbouring Southeast Asian countries will remain a distant aspiration. How can the Look East Policy generate incentives that can bring substantial changes in the political, socio-economic conditions of the people in the region? By raising this question, it would be meaningful for all of us to conceptualise the idea of "development" which the Look East Policy holds for the region. I am hopeful the preceding chapters will give a brief understanding of this.

Some of the contemporary scholars are optimistic about the Look East Policy. They believe that it will provide great opportunities for the region with the changing geopolitics of Asia. Many scholars argued that, "a transnational region across Indian eastern border could create the space for transnational politics of recognition that could respond to the urges prevalent in the region for recognition, apart from bringing about significant economic benefits."[6] On the contrary, many scholars argue that full-scale implementation of India's Look East Policy will certainly have a direct bearing on the issue of migration, both legal and illegal, in the Northeast. Scholars are critical of the fact that it would become increasingly difficult for the indigenous people of the Northeastern region to resist the civilian aggression once legal status is accorded to immigrants as a part of establishment of formal trade relations. Scholars are also of the opinion that, "as Indian exports to Southeast Asia comprises items not produced in the Northeast region, the logic of physical connectivity is solely seen in terms of providing a transit point."[7] Scholars are also critical of the policy of integrating Northeast India with its eastern neighbours as it would lead to dumping of cheap foreign goods and the region's own industries would be adversely affected by it.[8] Again, from the geostrategic perspective, Look East Policy also becomes more important in the present geopolitical reality with China's assertive posturing with regard to Arunachal Pradesh and construction of dams on the Brahmaputra river. Thus, we find that Look East Policy has both negative and positive understanding amongst the scholars working in the field. It is important in this context to discuss a few things about the North Eastern Region Vision 2020. As laid down clearly in the vision statement of North Eastern Region Vision 2020, "the purpose of The Northeast Region Vision 2020 is to return the North Eastern Region to the position of national economic eminence it held till a few decades ago; to so fashion the development process that growth springs from and spreads out to the grassroots; and to ensure that the Region plays the arrowhead role it must in the vanguard of the country's Look East Policy."[9] However, the Vision 2020 is being critiqued as, "the Vision promotes certain stereotypical ideas about Northeast through its economistic vision that fails to recognise the lived experiences of people."[10]

As India's LEP is also coming through the discourse of development, it is important to understand what the "Right to Development" means for the Northeast region which has been neglected for the past 65years. Needless to say, it is still continuing. There is no effort on the part of the Central and the State governments to involve the stakeholders in the process of development of the region in the line of India's Look East, or Act East Policy, as we call it today. Thus, it is important to understand that "without the right to participate, human societies are reduced to 'target groups' to be administered state-initiated policies and bureaucratic intervention."[11]

It may also be mentioned here that the North Eastern Council (NEC) and Ministry of Development of North Eastern Region (MDONER) are serving within the security framework of Government of India. These two bodies are making the local people less powerful. There is the need to analyse the kind of development the Indian state envisages for the NE, and which part is ignored by both NEC and MDONER. However, it is important today that the Central Government implement certain projects which will enhance people-to-people contact in the region. No such major policies have been seen till date within the framework of India's Act East Policy. Instead, on June 4, 2015 at least 20 soldiers were killed and 11 others injured in an ambush in Manipur's Chandel district. In response the Centre ordered an all-out offensive against the insurgents in the Northeast after the Manipur ambush. The Army has been asked to launch "search and destroy" operations against the militants.[12] This kind of decision will never solve the problems of the region. More comprehensive policies are required to solve the problem of insurgency.

It is time for everyone to understand that to facilitate investments in the region, a systematic understanding and mapping of people, their foundations, resources, etc., are to be made. Otherwise, the people of the Northeast region will not be able to relate themselves with the integration process set by the national and worldwide economic system on terms largely set by those outside the neighbourhood.[13] On the other hand, the government is allowing International Financial Institutions (IFIs) to operate in the region. Those IFIs have begun to disregard the rights of indigenous and tribal peoples to their land by seeking changes in existing legislation and policy to allow privatisation, corporate alliances and individual appropriation. In turn, the indigenous people have been criminalised for defending their lives and societies.

As studied by different groups during the survey conducted under the present project, the activities of IFIs in the Northeast have revealed the failure of development agencies, IFIs and governments to respect peoples' right to participation and self-determination. Violations of existing norms on human rights and policy standards have also been reported from the region. What is depicted is that there is no free flow of information, resulting in the people being unaware of implications that are coming in the name of development. And a critical observation of the working of IFIs and other state institutions reveals many critical voices, opinions and concerns. In recent times, infrastructural development like road building has been emphasised as a result of India's current Look East Policy, where road construction constitutes a top priority for State economic planners in order to link the region with a "progressive" global economy.[14] However, beyond the scope of road construction what many scholars have argued is that the image of Northeast region as being *plentiful, vulnerable and easily available* continues to entertain the fantasies of the Indian capitalist politico-security establishment.

Though the LEP promises a great deal for the region's development, the rise of drug use, HIV/AIDS and human trafficking has created a severe worry, as this involves the young income-earning population. Equally it has been noted that in any society where HIV/AIDS epidemics occur, the outgrowth and development are hindered with a slower increase in population and supply of labour due to AIDS-linked deaths. There is a fear that this can also cause a big impact on unskilled labour. Since in the case of Northeast region drug abuse, HIV/AIDS and human trafficking has been taking place, the occurrence of such effects will contribute to further illegal migration problem of labourers which will have ramifications on the socio-economic status of the masses. The bulk of development policies justified in the name of national interest has diminished the local people's ability to control and gainfully use their resources, and their right to development is violated. As agreed by most scholars, though the LEP promises a lot for the region, one should realise that sustainability and satisfaction of the people will not be brought about by technology, connectivity, and economy alone but by a political framework based on democratic values which can give people the local communities' rights over local issues, for example, land acquisition, building of dams, etc. The statist argument that fostering deeper economic and cultural and historical ties with the Southeast Asian countries will not only promote better economic opportunities for the region but also help in containing separatist movements is belied by ground realities. Udayon Misra contends that as assertions of identity often leading to insurgent movements had their roots in economic deprivation, these in turn, have acted as a major impediment to development. The economy of underdevelopment and colonial exploitation has been encouraged by the politics of alienation practised by the Centre.[15] Due to India's LEP, projects have been proposed for roads, dams, etc. But the government has neither any resettlement nor a rehabilitation policy for the present and the immediate future generations who are to be displaced,[16] which raises a deep concern. And if the Indian state continues and fails to understand the Northeast region and its people, the region will be once again trapped in the vicious cycle of underdevelopment and unrest.[17]

Observing the work done by the Indian Government through the years, a lot still needs to be done in integrating the region and its people with the rest of India. Till the government tries to fully integrate the Northeast region into the mainstream economy, both psychologically and economically, it will remain a mere transit point, as feared by some scholars, and the *trust-deficit* will continue. The efficient implementation of LEP requires clearing and interpreting the fears that it will bring about in society political, economic, societal and security worries, which means encouraging more scholarly work as the LEP or Act East Policy is still an ongoing task. Thus, Government strategy should aim at a cooperative solution involving all the state governments and sharing of information not only among governments, but also regional and subregional governing bodies, faculty members, researchers and civil society. The first steps to provide transparency have to be effectively utilised. Government must ensure that within the framework of liberalisation and globalisation, the interest of the poor and marginalised must be secured. And, as the Northeast is also economically backward, the Act East Policy which centres on market rationality may not be conducive for democratic institutions in the area. Thus, in any negotiation concerning the Northeast regional and subregional organisations, the Centre should ensure that the representatives of the region and their observations are properly respected. Government of India should make efforts to present the Act East Policy as a great opportunity for the people of the Northeast region and the Indian state to come closer and integrate politically, economically, psychologically, emotionally and physically. The state of political, socio-economic conditions—six decades old unresolved problems of insurgency, misgovernance, corruption, nonaccountability, militarisation and culture of impunity, lack of infrastructure in basic public delivery systems, including absence of reliable transport and communication facilities—must be sorted out immediately by giving proper respect to the stakeholders of the region. If the Indian state requires an effective Look East Policy or Act East Policy and tangible solutions, an accountable socio-economic policy and adequate mechanisms for the welfare of the people in the region should be offered. These include better infrastructure and safe and cheap health maintenance system, education, electrification, etc. Otherwise, chances are high that the people of the Northeastern region will face more survival threats in the near future concerning the political conflict between the Central government and non-state actors of the region. The real situation on the ground is that after more than 20 years, the LEP has not contributed anything substantial to the economic development of the NE. The conflicts in the region stay unresolved and positive peace remains elusive. Manipur, Nagaland and Assam remain potboilers of latent conflicts, erupting at different levels of violence from time to time. The other states, less violent, are equally afflicted by the narratives of underdevelopment and group identities. The LEP cannot turn a blind eye to the conflicts and let the prevailing turmoil render bypassing the NE an unavoidable logistical necessity. Central to this issue is the question of peace in Northeast India—positive peace that would be a contributory factor for the fruitful involvement of the region in the LEP. It seems to have been assumed that a greater economic participation resulting from the LEP would automatically remove much of the problems in Northeast India. That such an assumption can only result in the policy becoming a non-starter has been proven by the lethargic economic impact on the Northeast. Security-related issues ensuing from unresolved, protracted conflicts may become an alibi for bypassing the region. Even as the country projects itself to the neighbouring Southeast Asian nations, apparently, there is no expressed strategy in the LEP seeking to resolve the conflicts in the Northeast systematically. This lack of a methodical approach to peace and conflict resolution relegates to the periphery the involvement and engagement of the region in the LEP.

India's LEP can be substantiated only through Northeast India. The Northeast can be a hub of tourists, culture and trade activities. It is so important strategically that once Southeast Asia is linked by land to this region, India will gain not just in business terms but it would help integration of the country with nations of this region, culturally Northeast and Southeast Asia being so close. Today, India's Northeast stands at the edge of a new reality. Return of peace and imaginative planning can ensure a turnaround for the economy. Restoration of pre-Partition links with neighbouring countries can work wonders for trade and business. Resolution of the conflicts that have festered can set the stage for the creation of better transport and communication infrastructure. Multiplicity of identity is acceptable as long as it does not become a source of continuing conflict that saps the vitality of an otherwise vibrant region. Identity management and development of a political culture of tolerance are needed in the Northeast. Northeast India is one region that desperately needs an agenda of ethnic reconciliation that can be implemented both from the top and at the grassroots because, if ethnic conflicts intensify, people may step in to take advantage of the disturbed situation. Peace processes are highly complex with divergent interests, actors and emotions in play, made even more difficult due to the overarching factor of violence. In a conflict situation, the category of "friend" and "enemy" takes centre stage, with other identities relegated to the background, especially in areas where the conflict is wrapped around notions of ethnic identity.[18] As a result, the peace process in Northeast Region has to be handled carefully, without harming the interests of the local stakeholders. Only after the restoration of peace in the region will India's Northeast Imagination get a proper shape.

The limited perspective of the LEP symbolises an impoverished constitutionalism that turns Northeast India's responsible dissent into an "unrecognised ethnography" of everyday politics. One needs to understand how these limits are arrived at and further to what extent these limits meet the geopolitically Asian reality. The sense of political "insecurity" that we perceive in NEI today alternately creates "cultural insecurity." As a region of multiple transnational flows, imageries such as riverine and hilly terrains across Mekong delta to Chindwin and Irrawaddy to Tsiang, the Pang-Sau pass, Sela Pass and "Lake of No Return" assume a distinctive (hydro) geopolitical space which has to be understood by the policymakers of India. This method of connectivity has to be to be conceptualised here. An opening towards an exilic regionalism would bring together the unrepresented and unspoken Asiatic connections that include India's Northeast as a conjunction between South Asia and Southeast Asia has to be dealt seriously and with the sense of passion. The subregional contour of ASEAN, SAARC, IORARC, BIMSTEC, BRICS and many other such future bi- and multilateral formations needs to be explored through spaces and territories that were rarely paid attention to in the past. Following comparative methodologies of area studies and transboundary character of subregional formations, it is possible to build an ontology of dynamics of flow and control in the region. On the other hand, the process of subregionalism would transform existing rivalry structures and military competition into a bulwark of multi-state multi-partner sharing of resources and knowledge. One would also mark out the dichotomy between India's agenda-setting policy formalism of security and development mix that gets subverted from within the corridors of power. Such formalism faces the daunting task of managing a porous border by turning it into the soft border that Asiatic subregional interconnections demand. India's vertical top-down multiscalar ontology local-subnational-national matrix of policymaking and agenda-setting is not only disabled to perform such a task in the cusp region of the Northeast, but it is yet to articulate a horizontal pathway of linking up factors and actors who are themselves arranged historically in a civilisational cusp in their linkages with South and Southeast Asia. It is to be noted here that the BIMSTEC process has made steady progress over the brief years of its existence. The hosting of the second Summit in New Delhi in 2008 by India and two Ministerial Meetings during the last three years has helped the process move forward. Important milestones have also been achieved during India's Chairmanship of BIMSTEC, including the finalisation of the Convention on Combating International Terrorism and the Memorandum of Association for the Establishment of Cultural Industries Commission and Observatory, the Energy Centre and Centre for Weather and Climate. It is now important that BIMSTEC cooperation should also be accelerated in the other agreed priority areas such as energy, fisheries, agriculture, public health, poverty alleviation, counterterrorism and transnational crime, environment and natural disaster management.

The Kunming Initiative or BCIM

The Kunming Initiative, or what has come to be known as BCIM (Bangladesh, China, India and Myanmar) Forum, is one such subregional venture to explore the prospects of cooperation by clustering parts or whole of Bangladesh, China, India and Myanmar, specifically the landlocked frontier areas.[19] The term subregional is used because all the four countries Bangladesh, China, India and Myanmar are members of one or more regional associations. Besides, subregionalism is assumed to be more expedient "when integration of entire economies and regions proves limited and fraught with difficulties," and countries then work together to make "growth polygons" based on "particular transnational but contiguous areas."[20] The seven states of Northeast India and Yunnan Province in South-West China had much to gain from this subregional cooperation. For the members of BCIM, the interest was to access the benefits of BCIM cooperation through better connectivity and higher flows of trade in goods and services. The BCIM Forum, which began as a Track II initiative, is now gradually moving towards Track I. Fortunately, the BCIM initiative has been sustained for more than a decade now. With the commitment demonstrated in Kunming initially, the four countries are approaching a stage where many of the promising ideas of cooperation, which were articulated when the Forum was set up, have started to take a concrete shape. The success of BCIM forum, like any other subregional cooperation project will depend on political, economic, cultural, and administrative institutionalised practices and social consciousness, and continually reproduced in these practices. As Northeast India shares 98 per cent of its border with Myanmar, Bangladesh, China and Bhutan, building transport and trading corridors at various border points can offer essential subsistence items at much cheaper terms. Because of the transport cost involved, people in the region pay almost double the price for goods coming from industrial metros like Delhi, Mumbai and Kolkata. Opening of transport connectivity and trading routes within the BCIM neighbourhood can substantially relieve the burden in the frontiers of Northeast India, whose market turnover is estimated at US$ 50 billion. BCIM Forum countries include two of the largest economies of the world, namely, China and India, which are expected to be key economic players in the twenty-first century, as discussed earlier in this article. This offers significant new opportunities for the other two countries of the region, i.e., Bangladesh and Myanmar, to take advantage of the growing market, investible finance and technological resources of both China and India. Bangladesh and Myanmar may also try to benefit from the active policies of economic cooperation of China and India with countries of ASEAN and Africa. New developments in Myanmar's economic and financial policy regime promise to add dynamism to the above-mentioned possibilities within the structure of BCIM. Of particular interest the current juncture are the important and significant changes that are taking place in present-day Myanmar. The evolving scenario in Myanmar is characterised by opening up of its economy through liberalisation of trade and Foreign Direct Investment (FDI) regimes. These measures are likely to create a supportive environment for greater regional cooperation in exploitation of natural resources (particularly energy resources) as well as putting in place more effective trade facilitation and multi-modal connectivity. There are several other areas that were recently pointed out in the 11th BCIM Forum held in Dhaka in February 2013. As a part of this BCIM forum a car rally was also organised from Kolkata to Kunming which was flagged off in Kolkata on February 22, 2013 and had been flagged off on March 5, 2013 at Kunming by the Vice Governor of Yunnan Province in South-West China.

Home to about forty per cent of the world's population, the region could derive further benefits had it opted for forging closer cooperation through trade and investment complementarities. Sure enough, there is a need for expending serious effort towards identifying how one country's export profile matches with the import profile of another country within this group. Trade and investment plan can thus be based on mutual demands for products and commodities, industrial base, transfer of technology and supply of energy or power and raw materials. Ethnologically advanced as China and India are, they seem to be more concerned about looking for markets for their products.[21]

It is to be mentioned here that one of the reasons why the South Asian Association for Regional Cooperation (SAARC) did not take off is the political mistrust. The emerging nations in the region consider themselves competitors to each other and hence the strategic consideration gets the better of economic collaboration. If the nations were determined to bolster economic cooperation allowing access commodities duty-free or at nominal tariffs, they had to develop the communications network. The recent emphasis on this issue is not without interest. The Northeastern states of the Indian republic are too far from the centre of power in Delhi, so is the Yunnan province in South-West China. India needs direct routes to NEI and Yunnan seeks to have access to India through Assam. This is only possible if BCIM emerges as a powerful subregional organisation. Sometimes, countries within a regional forum seems to be more interested in state-to-state financial deals, showing trust to some of the member countries and mistrust to other members. This kind of attitude must be avoided. For example, a few companies from Bangladesh might be interested in setting up their agro-processing plants in the Northeastern Indian states to both sides' benefit. Such cooperation does not materialise because none of the forum members seems to appreciate the merit of complementarity when it comes to interregional trade and investment. It is thus important while framing the subregional groupings that mutual trust must be enhanced.

The contributory factor within the structure of BCIM of course is the economic dynamism of the two most populous countries in the world. But if they pressed for subregional trade integration, they had better make a mind to follow the model pursued by Taiwan and Hong Kong, who together shared the task of supplying manufacturing components and providing services sector facilities for industrial development in Guangdong and Fujian provinces. Here is a growth triangle that derived the driving force behind it from market forces and private sector initiatives. A similar growth triangle in the shape of Singapore's relocation of its plants in the neighbouring areas of Indonesia and Malaysia has emerged or is emerging in Southeast Asia. Such positive developments can now act as an inspiration for both India and China for development of industries in both Myanmar and Bangladesh, in the NEIs or in the mid-South-Western region of China.

With two of the economies going strong, a third one not lagging far behind and a fourth one now opening up its economy, the BCIM surely needs to focus on developing a growth quadrangle involving NEIs, mid-South-Western China, Myanmar and Bangladesh. If the plan for making business enterprises at the confluence goes strongly through mutual cooperation, road or rail communications can simultaneously be developed with the aim of taking the load of augmented commerce and business. In a world where economic compulsion is proving overriding, no strategic consideration—be it military or political—should blur the vision. The leaderships of the region should now set their sights beyond those horizons in favour of trade and investment.[22] At the same time, the member countries must be cautious enough of the fact that deregulation and liberalisation processes must be handled with care, because there is always the threat of the most powerful countries of the world on the economies of the developing world. It is true that K2K initiative is a good initiative for both the nations, but will China approve this kind of route in any other areas where it is sharing borders with India? The probable answer is "no." China will only approve those routes where its own interest lies, and India must again be careful on these issues. As far as my perception goes, India cannot just deal with China from an idealistic point of view. India has to be realistic in dealing with China.

BIMSTEC is an important vehicle to promote regional cooperation and economic integration in a range of areas in South Asia. It is also important for us to develop BIMSTEC as a vibrant organisation which will be able to make Northeast India as the gateway to Southeast Asia. This will make India's "Look East Policy" much more empirical. The success of BIMSTEC will definitely contribute and complement the development of India's Look East Policy/Act East Policy, in general, and Northeast, in particular. Indeed, for India, this regional grouping acts as a medium for achieving the three-pronged strategy of its Look East Policy: (a) closer link with its proximate and immediate neighbours, (b) economic integration with Southeast Asia, and (c) security considerations of Northeast India and development of its untapped potential. Various infrastructural efforts will be enhanced with the participation of the member countries which in turn will also bring out reciprocal benefits. An effective and progressive cooperation is very much in demand between BIMSTEC and Northeast India in the present century. BIMSTEC has, over the years, identified wide and diverse range sectors for cooperation. Considerable progress has been achieved in some of the focus areas of cooperation. Taking satisfaction from this, much needs to be done. BIMSTEC is a grouping with immense potential. It is important for the BIMSTEC nations to work more closely for fuller realisation of its potential. India remains committed to continue its full engagement with BIMSTEC partners for strengthening the grouping and realising its goals. In recent years the challenge for India has been to influence the thinking on globalisation, to reshape it, to reduce the chances of it going awry and destroying economies and countries. The emerging relations between India and BIMSTEC countries will show the world that the dominant pattern of international politics is therefore produced through the machinations and operations of most of the developing nations, not as passive dependencies but as active partners in a global strategy of domination. On the other hand it is evident that the present-day notion of accepting South and Southeast Asia as a "principal market" by the major players in the world will give new direction to India's "Look East Policy/Act East Policy." India will undoubtedly energise its "Look East Policy/Act East Policy" to give shape to the idea of "Asian Century." It is important for India to increase its intellectual and diplomatic involvement in East and Southeast Asia to give proper shape to its Look East Policy. It is only through this policy that it will be possible for India to emerge as a major power in the Asia-Pacific and Southeast Asia. It is important for India to develop a vision of its own economic future and a vision of its future strategic role in the region. This is because East Asia and Southeast Asia are becoming an increasingly crowded strategic space for India. The admission of the United States and Russia to the East Asia Summit during its meeting in Indonesia in November 2011could make it increasingly difficult for India to make its voice heard in the region. This comes as Russia is reasserting its position as a provider of military hardware and energy assistance to the region. Meanwhile, the United States has reasserted its role of "strategic balancer" and protector of the global commons by reaffirming its bilateral alliance relationships in the region, most notably with Japan, South Korea and the Philippines, which have all had recent tensions with China. The "Great Power" competition in the region is emerging due to the rise of a new multipolar international order in which the United States, while the dominant player, will increasingly be challenged in the economic, political and security arenas by a more aggressive and confident China, a revised state like Russia, and more independently acting Japan and Europe, along with smaller countries that will also take part in the competition over strategically important resources like oil and gas, iron ore and other minerals, or related important resources such as sea lanes, airspace, and the environment. Given the condition of India's burgeoning resource needs and the need to sustain its development and growth targets through attracting foreign investment and accessing the rapidly growing markets of East Asia and Southeast Asia, India must rejuvenate its "Look East Policy" to ensure that it remains a major player in this region of growing strategic importance. To implement this, India will need to take its engagement with East Asia and Southeast Asia beyond mere interaction and confidence-building toward integration, agenda-setting and conflict resolution. This will automatically help the Northeast India to experience growth, peace and prosperity. This, however, depends on India's foreign policy success in Myanmar, something that is never guaranteed, given the economic, political and strategic stakes involved. While China has invested in business and infrastructure development in Myanmar in a big way, India's parallel policy has been sluggish and lacklustre. Peace and stability on the Indian side of the frontier is also a vital precondition for this. While the political situation in the Northeast, barring a few isolated pockets, is much improved compared to the past, the costs of peace are exorbitant for all stakeholders in the process. On a more concrete note, the Government of India needs to do several things to recharge and redeploy its LEP with an eye to reaping benefits for the Northeast. First, it needs to freely talk to and patiently hear the voices of the ordinary people of the Northeast, no matter what these views are. Without articulating a new geography of extended neighbourhood, there is little hope that the economic benefits accruing out of LEP will reach the people of the Northeast. Second, India needs to link up more effectively with the supply chain economies of Southeast Asia that are looking for new markets since the global recession has set in. A growth triangle connecting South-Western China, India's Northeast and Southeast Asia promises immense economic benefits to all stakeholders if political differences are carefully negotiated. Third, there is an immediate need to complete some of the infrastructural projects that link India with Southeast Asia through Myanmar. Without good roads, there cannot be any economic development of the region. Fourth, India needs to consolidate its diplomatic gains in Myanmar and improve ties at all levels. In recent years India, along with China and the Association of Southeast Asian Nations (ASEAN), has been following a policy of diplomatic and strategic engagement with Myanmar. India, in this situation, cannot opt out. Thus, India's present policy has been framed to serve its own interests having relevance to its Northeast, to counterbalance the increasing Chinese influence in Myanmar and to address security conditions. To conclude, it is important to say that it is now time for India to take advantage of the emerging possibilities of its "Look East Policy"/"Act East Policy."

Notes

1. Jadav Pegu, "Does India's Look East Policy Bypass peace in the North East?" in Imankalyan Lahiri and Pahi Saikia (eds.), *North East in India's Look East: Issues and Opportunities* (Bharti Publications: New Delhi, 2015), pp. 92-100.
2. Yashwant Singh, as quoted in S. Kumara, "Burma visit highlights India's 'Look East' strategy," April 6, 2005.
   Retrieved from: http://www.wsws.org/articules/2005/apr2005/indi-a06.shtml.
3. Closing statement of Shri Pranab Mukherjee at Look East Policy meeting on October 31, 2007.

4. Caroline Maninee, "India's Look East Policy and the North East Region: A Perspective," in Lahiri and Saikia (eds.), *North East in India's Look East...*, pp. 1-16.
5. Manmohan Singh, "PM's address at the inauguration of New Capital Complex of Assam," Dispur, November 21, 2004.
6. Cited in n. 3, Sanjib Baruah, *Durable Disorder: Understanding the Politics of Northeast India* (New Delhi: OUP, 2005), p. 232.
7. Oinam Bhagat, "Manipur" in Mayumi Mayurama (ed.), *Sub-Regional Relations in the Eastern South Asia: With Special Focus on India's North Eastern Region* (Chiba: IDE-JETRO, 2005), p. 105.
8. G. Parthasarathy, "Look beyond 'look east,'" *The Pioneer*, December 21, 2000.
9. *North Eastern Region Vision 2020.* Ministry of Development of North East Region and North Eastern Council, 2008.
10. Prasenjit Biswas, "Post-Development, Democratic Discourse and Dissensus: A Critique of Vision 2020," *Eastern Quarterly*, vol. 4, issues III and IV, October 2007-2008, p. 186.
11. Ajay Gudavarthy, "Human Rights," in Bhupinder S. Chimni and Siddharth Mallavarapu, *International Relations: Perspectives for the Global South,* p. 399.
12. Manipur Ambush, "Centre orders 'search and destroy' operations," *The Citizen Bureau,* Sunday, June 7, 2015.
13. Ramananda Wangkheirakpam and Jiten Yumnam, "Insidious Financial Intrusions in India's Northeast," Intercultural Resources and Forum for Indigenous Perspectives and Action, April 2006. (Retrieved from http://www.icrindia.org/pdf/IFI_in_North East_India.pdf, p. 6.)
14. Lipokmar, Dzuvichu, "How many Roads must the State Build? Revisiting a regions's developmental puzzle: An Essay," Biblio, Volume XIII, Nos: 5 & 6, (May-June 2008), p. 30.
15. Udayon Misra, *The Periphery Strikes Back: Challenges to the Nation-State in Assam and Nagaland* (Shimla: Indian Institute of Advanced Studies, 2000).
16. Monirul Hussain, *Interrogating Development: State, Displacement and Popular Resistance in North East India* (New Delhi: Sage Publications, 2008), p. 40.
17. Ibid., p. 153.
18. Amit Ron, "Peace Negotiations and Peace Talks: The Peace Process in the Public Sphere," *International Journal of Peace Studies*, 14/1, Spring/Summer, 2009 at http://www.gmu.edu/programs/icar/ijps/vol14_1/Ron14n1IJPS.pdf (Accessed on September 13, 2013).
19. P. V. Indiresan, "Regional Cooperation: Kunming Initiative," *Frontline*, vol. 17, April 1-14, 2000.
20. Jenina Joy and Chavez-Malaluan, "Co-opting Cooperation: The Asian Development Bank and Sub-regional Economic Zone," available at: www.forum-adb.org/unsorted/srez.pdf, p. 1.
21. Only recently did a conglomerate of India, Tatas, come forward with a proposal for big investment.
22. Nilratan Haldar, "Developing a BCIM growth quadrangle," in *The Financial Express*, March 1, 2013.

BIBLIOGRAPHY

A Handbook of Anthropology. Noida: Orient BlackSwan, 2012.

Aglaja, Stirn and Ham van Peter. *The Seven Sisters of India: Tribal Worlds between Tibet and Burma*. Ahmedabad: Mapin Publishing, 2000.

Ahmed, Rafiul and Prasenjit Biswas. *Political Economy of Underdevelopment of Northeast India*. New Delhi: Akansha Publishing House, 2004.

Ambrose, Pinto. "Basic Conflict of 'We' and 'They' between Social and Ethnic Groups," in Imtiaz Ahmad, Partha S. Ghosh and Helmut Reifeld (eds.), *Pluralism and Equality: Values in Indian Society and Politics*. New Delhi: Sage Publications, pp. 180-196, 2000.

Baruah, Apura Kumar. *Social Tensions in Assam: Middle Class Politics*. Guwahati: Purbanchal Prakashan, 1991.

Bhagabati, A. C. "Tribal transformation in Assam and North East India: An appraisal of emerging ideological dimensions." Presidential Address, Section of Anthropology and Archaeology, Seventy-fifth Indian Science Congress, Pune. Calcutta: Indian Science Congress Association, 1988.

Bhagabati, A. C. 1992. "Social formation in Noth East India." *Bulletin of the Department of Anthropology*, Gauhati University, VI: 9-29, 1992.

Biswas, Prasenjit and Chandan Suklabaidya. *Ethnic Life-Worlds in northeast India*. New Delhi: Sage Publications, 2001.

Bose, Partha Pratim, ed. *State, Nation and Democracy: Shifting Alignments*. New Delhi: Concept Publishing Company, 2007, pp. 246-83.

Brass, Paul R. *Ethnicity and Nationalism: Theory and Comparison*. New Delhi: Sage Publications, 1991.

Brown, M. E. *Ethnic Conflict and International Security*. Princeton, N. J.: Princeton University Press, 1993.

Chasie, C. *The Naga Imbroglio (A Personal Perspective)*. Kohima: Standard Printers & Publishers, 2000.

Chaterji, Suniti Kumar. 1974. *Kirata-jana-Kriti*. Calcutta: Asiatic Society of Bengal, 1974.

Chazan, N., R. Mortimer, J. Ravenhill and D. Rothchild. *Politics and Society in Contemporary Africa*. Boulder: Colorado, Lynne Rienner Publications, 1998.

Das, B. M. *Anthropometry of the Tribal groups of Assam, India*. Florida: Field Research Project, 1970.

Das, B. M. *Ethnic Affinities of the Rabhas*. Guwahati: Gauhati University, 1960.

Dixit, J. N. *Makers of India's Foreign Policy*. New Delhi: HarperCollins Publishers, 2004.

Egreteau, R. *Instability at the Gate: India's Northeast and its External Connections*. New Delhi: Centre de Sciences Humaines, 2006.

Elwin, V. *Nagaland*. Shillong: Government of Nagaland, 1961.

Elwin, V. *The Nagas in Nineteenth Century*. London: Oxford University Press, 1969.

Fernandes, Walter. "Limits of Law and Order: Approach to the northeast." *Economic and Political Weekly*, Vol. XXXIX, No. 42, October 16, (2004): pp. 4609-4611.

Furer-Haimendorf, C. von. *The Naked Nagas*. Calcutta: Thacker, Spink & Co., 1962.

Ghurye, G. S. *The Scheduled Tribes of India*. Bombay: Popular Prakashan, 1963.

Gurr, Ted Robert. 1970. *Why Men Rebel?* Princeton: Princeton University Press, 1970.

Haopik, T. "Conceptualising Northeast India: A Discursive Analysis on Diversity." *e-journal of Sociology*, Vol. 8. No. 2, (2001): pp. 109-120, available at http://www.bangladeshsociology.org/BEJS%208.2%20Conceptualising%20Northeast%20India.pdf (Accessed on August 8, 2014).

Heredia, Rudolf C. 1997. "Ethnicity, Class and Nation: Interrelationships in a Multicultural State." *Economic and Political Weekly*, Vol. XXXII, No. 19, May 10, pp. 1010-1015.

Hiren, Gohain. 1997. "Ethnic Unrest in the northeast." *Economic and Political Weekly*, Vol. XXXII, No. 8, February 22 (1997): pp. 389-91.

Hodson, T. C. *The Naga Tribes of Manipur*. Delhi: B. R. Publishing Corporation, 1982.

Horam, M. *Naga Polity*. Delhi: B. R. Publishing Corporation, 1975.

Hutton, J. H. *The Angami Nagas*. London: Macmillan, 1921.

Hutton, J. H. *The Sema Nagas*. Bombay: Oxford University Press, 1990.

Kamei, G. *Ethnicity and Social Change: An Anthology of Essays*. New Delhi: Akansha Publishing House, 2008.

Lahiri, Imankalyan and Pahi Saikia. *North East in India's Look East: Issues and Opportunities*. New Delhi: Bharti Publications, 2015.

Lahiri, Imankalyan. *Malaysia's Foreign Policy: under Mahathir Mohammad*. New Delhi: Academic Excellence, 2009, pp. 167-78.

Madhab, Jayanta. "Northeast: Crisis of Identity, Security and Underdevelopment." *Economic and Political Weekly*, Vol. XXXIV, No. 6, February 6 (1999): pp. 320-22.

Majumdar, D. N. "North East India: A Profile." In T. C. Sharma and D. N. Majumdar, eds. *Eastern Himalayas*. New Delhi: Cosmo Publications, 1979.

Mills, J. P. *The Ao Nagas*. London: Macmillan,.1922.

Milton, Yinger J. *Ethnicity: Source of Strength? Source of Conflict?* Jaipur and New Delhi: Rawat Publications, 1997.

Misalucha, Charmaine G. "Southeast Asia-US Relations: Hegemony or Hierarchy." *Contemporary Southeast Asia*, Vol. 33, No. 2, August 2011, pp. 209-27.

Misra, Udoyon. "Assam: Roll-call of the Dead." *Economic and Political Weekly*, Vol. XXXVII, No. 37, September 14, pp. 3781-3785 (2002).

Misra, Udoyon. *The Periphery Strikes Back: Challenges to the Nation-State in Assam and Nagaland.* Shimla: Indian Institute of Advanced Study, 2000.

Muni, S. D. "India's Look East Policy: The Strategic Dimension." ISAS Working Paper, No. 121-1. February 2011.

Oommen, T. K. "Culture Change among the Tribes of northeast India." In T. B. Subba, Joseph Puthenpurakal and Shaji Joseph Puykunnel, eds. *Christianity and Change in Northeast India.* New Delhi: Concept Publishing Company, 2002.

Oommen, T. K. *Citizenship, Nationality and Ethnicity: Reconciling Competing Identities.* Cambridge: Polity Press, 1997.

Oommen, T. K., ed, Social Movements II: Concerns of Equality and Security (New Delhi: Oxford University Press, 2010).

Pathy, J. *Ethnic Minorities in the Process of Development.* Jaipur: Rawat Publications, 1988.

Power and W. J. Wilson. *Social Exclusion and the Future of Cities.* London: Centre for Analysis of Social Exclusion, School of Economics, 2000.

Rawls, John. *A Theory of Justice.* Cambridge: The Belknap Press of Harvard University, 1971.

Reddy, K. Raja, ed. *India and ASEAN: Foreign Policy Dimensions for the 21st Century.* New Delhi: New Century Publications, 2005, pp. 1-11, 201-2.

Roy Burman, B. K. 1970. *Demographic and Socioeconomic Profiles of the Hill Areas of North East India.* New Delhi: Office of the Registrar General of India, 1970.

Roy Burman, B. K. *Tribes in Prespective.* Delhi: Mittal Publications, 1994.

Roy, Sanjay K. "Conflicting Nations in northeast India." *Economic and Political Weekly*, Vol. XXXX, No. 21, May 21-27, 2005.

Saikia, Pahi. *Ethnic Mobilisation and Violence in Northeast India.* London: Routledge, 2011.

Sen, Amartya. *Identity and Violence: The Illusion of Destiny.* London: Penguin Books, 2006.

Sen, Rabindra and Suchita Ghosh, eds. *Southeast Asia: Security in the Coming Millennium.* Calcutta: Allied Publishers Limited, 2000, pp.102-17.

Sharma, Manorama. *Social and Economic Change in Assam: Middle Class Hegemony.* New Delhi: Ajanta Publications, 1990.

Singh, B. P. *The Problem of Change: A Study of Northeast India.* Delhi: Oxford University Press, 1998.

Singh, K. S. 1995. *People of India: Mizoram, XXXIII.* Calcutta: Anthropological Survey of India, 1995.

Singh, K. S. 1996. *People of India: Tripura, XLI.* Calcutta: Anthropological Survey of India, 1996.

Singh, K. S. 1998. *People of India: Manipur, XXXI.* Calcutta: Anthropological Survey of India, 1998.

Singh, K. S. *People of India: Arunachal Pradesh, XIV.* Calcutta: Anthropological Survey of India, 1995.

Singh, K. S. *People of India: Nagaland, XXXIV.* Calcutta: Anthropological Survey of India, 1994.

Singh, K. S. *Tribal Movements in India.* New Delhi: Manohar, 2006.

Smith, Anthony D. *Myths and Memories of the Nation.* Oxford: Oxford University Press, 1999.

Smith, Anthony D. *National Identity.* Reno: University of Nevada Press, 1993.

Srikanth, H. "Militancy and Identity Politics in Assam." *Economic and Political Weekly*, Vol. XXXV, No. 47, pp. 4117-4124 (2000).

Subba, T. B., ed. *North-East India: A Handbook of Anthropology.* Noida: Orient BlackSwan, 2012.

Taher, M. "Tribes in North East India: A diagnostic survey in spatial pattern." *The North East Geographer.* IX (1,2): 16-26 (1977).

Taylor, C. "The dynamics of democratic exclusion." *Journal of Democracy*, Vol. 9, No. 4, pp. 143-56 (1998).

Thong, Joseph S. 2012. *Head-Hunters Culture: Historic Culture of Nagas.* New Delhi: Mittal Publications, 2012.

Wdanga, Noyoo. "Ethnicity and Development in Sub-Saharan Africa." *Journal of Social Development in Africa*, Vol. 15, No. 2, July (2000), Oxford University Press, 2002.

Wimmer, Andres. "Ethnic Exclusion in Nationalising States." In Gerard Delanty and Krishan Kumar, eds. *The Sage Handbook of Nations and Nationalism.* London: Sage Publications, 2006, pp. 334-44.

Wolf, Marshall. "Globalisation and Social Exclusion: Some Paradoxes." In Gerry Rodgers, Charles Gore, Jose B. Figueiredo, eds. *Social Exclusion: Rhetoric, Reality, Responses*. Geneva: ILO, 1995.

Wolf, Stefan. *Ethnic Conflict: A Global Perspective*. Oxford: Oxford University Press, 2006.

Xaxa, V. *State, Society, and Tribes: Issues in Post-Colonial India*. New Delhi: Pearson Longman, 2008.

Zariski, Raphael. "Ethnic Extremism among Ethnoterritorial Minorities in Western Europe: Dimensions, Causes and Institutional Responses." *Comparative Politics*, Vol. 21, No. 3, April 1989.